No Lex 10-12

Juan Ponce de León

CONSULTING EDITORS

RODOLFO CARDONA

professor of Spanish and comparative literature,
Boston University

JAMES COCKCROFT

visiting professor of Latin American and Caribbean studies,
State University of New York at Albany

Juan Ponce de León

Sean Dolan

CHELSEA HOUSE PUBLISHERS
NEW YORK ■ PHILADELPHIA

CHELSEA HOUSE PUBLISHERS

Editorial Director: Richard Rennert
Executive Managing Editor: Karyn Gullen Browne
Copy Chief: Robin James
Picture Editor: Adrian G. Allen
Creative Director: Robert Mitchell
Art Director: Joan Ferrigno
Production Manager: Sallye Scott

HISPANICS OF ACHIEVEMENT
Senior Editor: Philip Koslow

Staff for *JUAN PONCE DE LEÓN*
Editorial Assistant: Annie McDonnell
Designer: M. Cambraia Magalhães
Picture Researcher: Sandy Jones

First Printing
1   3   5   7   9   8   6   4   2

Library of Congress Cataloging-in-Publication Data
Dolan, Sean.
Juan Ponce de León/Sean Dolan.
p. cm.—(Hispanics of achievement)
Includes bibliographical references and index.
ISBN 0-7910-2023-1
ISBN 0-7910-2024-X (pbk.)
1. Ponce de León, Juan, 1460?–1521—Juvenile literature. 2. Explorers—America—Bi-
ography—Juvenile literature. 3. Explorers—Spain—Biography—Juvenile literature. 4.
America—Discovery and exploration—Spanish—Juvenile literature. [1. Ponce de
León, Juan 1460?–1521. 2. Explorers. 3. America—Discovery and exploration—Span-
ish.] I. Title. II. Series.
95-20
E125.P7D65 1995
CIP
972.9'02'092—dc20
AC
[B]

CONTENTS

Hispanics of Achievement   7

First Citizen of a New World   15

An Interesting Age   25

To the New World   37

Conquering Hispaniola   51

Borinquén and Becerillo   71

To Live Forever   87

Chronology   105

Further Reading   107

Index   108

JOAN BAEZ
Mexican-American folksinger

RUBÉN BLADES
Panamanian lawyer and entertainer

JORGE LUIS BORGES
Argentine writer

PABLO CASALS
Spanish cellist and conductor

MIGUEL DE CERVANTES
Spanish writer

CESAR CHAVEZ
Mexican-American labor leader

JULIO CÉSAR CHÁVEZ
Mexican boxing champion

EL CID
Spanish military leader

HENRY CISNEROS
Mexican-American political leader

ROBERTO CLEMENTE
Puerto Rican baseball player

SALVADOR DALÍ
Spanish painter

PLÁCIDO DOMINGO
Spanish singer

GLORIA ESTEFAN
Cuban-American singer

GABRIEL GARCÍA MÁRQUEZ
Colombian writer

FRANCISCO JOSÉ DE GOYA
Spanish painter

JULIO IGLESIAS
Spanish singer

RAUL JULIA
Puerto Rican actor

FRIDA KAHLO
Mexican painter

JOSÉ MARTÍ
Cuban revolutionary and poet

RITA MORENO
Puerto Rican singer and actress

PABLO NERUDA
Chilean poet and diplomat

OCTAVIO PAZ
Mexican poet and critic

PABLO PICASSO
Spanish artist

ANTHONY QUINN
Mexican-American actor

DIEGO RIVERA
Mexican painter

LINDA RONSTADT
Mexican-American singer

ANTONIO LÓPEZ DE SANTA ANNA
Mexican general and politician

GEORGE SANTAYANA
Spanish philosopher and poet

JUNÍPERO SERRA
Spanish missionary and explorer

LEE TREVINO
Mexican-American golfer

PANCHO VILLA
Mexican revolutionary

C H E L S E A   H O U S E   P U B L I S H E R S

HISPANICS OF ACHIEVEMENT

Rodolfo Cardona

The Spanish language and many other elements of Spanish culture are present in the United States today and have been since the country's earliest beginnings. Some of these elements have come directly from the Iberian Peninsula; others have come indirectly, by way of Mexico, the Caribbean basin, and the countries of Central and South America.

Spanish culture has influenced America in many subtle ways, and consequently many Americans remain relatively unaware of the extent of its impact. The vast majority of them recognize the influence of Spanish culture in America, but they often do not realize the great importance and long history of that influence. This is partly because Americans have tended to judge the Hispanic influence in the United States in statistical terms rather than to look closely at the ways in which individual Hispanics have profoundly affected American culture. For this reason, it is fitting that Americans obtain more than a passing acquaintance with the origins of these Spanish cultural elements and gain an understanding of how they have been woven into the fabric of American society.

It is well documented that Spanish seafarers were the first to explore and colonize many of the early territories of what is today called the United States of America. For this reason, stu-

dents of geography discover Hispanic names all over the map of
the United States. For instance, the Strait of Juan de Fuca was
named after the Spanish explorer who first navigated the waters
of the Pacific Northwest; the names of states such as Arizona (arid
zone), Montana (mountain), Florida (thus named because it was
reached on Easter Sunday, which in Spanish is called the feast of
Pascua Florida), and California (named after a fictitious land in
one of the first and probably the most popular among the Spanish
novels of chivalry, *Amadis of Gaul*) are all derived from Spanish;
and there are numerous mountains, rivers, canyons, towns, and
cities with Spanish names throughout the United States.

Not only explorers but many other illustrious figures in
Spanish history have helped define American culture. For example, the 13th-century king of Spain, Alfonso X, also known as
the Learned, may be unknown to the majority of Americans, but
his work on the codification of Spanish law has greatly influenced
the evolution of American law, particularly in the jurisdictions of
the Southwest. For this contribution a statue of him stands in the
rotunda of the Capitol in Washington, D.C. Likewise, the name
Diego Rivera may be unfamiliar to most Americans, but this
Mexican painter influenced many American artists whose paint-
ings, commissioned during the Great Depression and the New
Deal era of the 1930s, adorn the walls of government buildings
throughout the United States. In recent years the contributions of
Puerto Ricans, Mexicans, Mexican Americans (Chicanos), and
Cubans in American cities such as Boston, Chicago, Los Angeles,
Miami, Minneapolis, New York, and San Antonio have been
enormous.

The importance of the Spanish language in this vast cultural
complex cannot be overstated. Spanish, after all, is second only to
English as the most widely spoken of Western languages within
the United States as well as in the entire world. The popularity of
the Spanish language in America has a long history.

In addition to Spanish exploration of the New World, the
great Spanish literary tradition served as a vehicle for bringing the

language and culture to America. Interest in Spanish literature in America began when English immigrants brought with them translations of Spanish masterpieces of the Golden Age. As early as 1683, private libraries in Philadelphia and Boston contained copies of the first picaresque novel, *Lazarillo de Tormes*, translations of Francisco de Quevedo's *Los Sueños*, and copies of the immortal epic of reality and illusion *Don Quixote*, by the great Spanish writer Miguel de Cervantes. It would not be surprising if Cotton Mather, the arch-Puritan, read *Don Quixote* in its original Spanish, if only to enrich his vocabulary in preparation for his writing *La fe del cristiano en 24 artículos de la Institución de Cristo, enviada a los españoles para que abran sus ojos* (The Christian's Faith in 24 Articles of the Institution of Christ, Sent to the Spaniards to Open Their Eyes), published in Boston in 1699.

Over the years, Spanish authors and their works have had a vast influence on American literature—from Washington Irving, John Steinbeck, and Ernest Hemingway in the novel to Henry Wadsworth Longfellow and Archibald MacLeish in poetry. Such important American writers as James Fenimore Cooper, Edgar Allan Poe, Walt Whitman, Mark Twain, and Herman Melville all owe a sizable debt to the Spanish literary tradition. Some writers, such as Willa Cather and Maxwell Anderson, who explored Spanish themes they came into contact with in the American Southwest and Mexico, were influenced less directly but no less profoundly.

Important contributions to a knowledge of Spanish culture in the United States were also made by many lesser known individuals—teachers, publishers, historians, entrepreneurs, and others—with a love for Spanish culture. One of the most significant of these contributions was made by Abiel Smith, a Harvard College graduate of the class of 1764, when he bequeathed stock worth $20,000 to Harvard for the support of a professor of French and Spanish. By 1819 this endowment had produced enough income to appoint a professor, and the philologist and humanist George Ticknor became the first holder of the Abiel

Smith Chair, which was the very first endowed Chair at Harvard University. Other illustrious holders of the Smith Chair would include the poets Henry Wadsworth Longfellow and James Russell Lowell.

A highly respected teacher and scholar, Ticknor was also a collector of Spanish books, and as such he made a very special contribution to America's knowledge of Spanish culture. He was instrumental in amassing for Harvard libraries one of the first and most impressive collections of Spanish books in the United States. He also had a valuable personal collection of Spanish books and manuscripts, which he bequeathed to the Boston Public Library.

With the creation of the Abiel Smith Chair, Spanish language and literature courses became part of the curriculum at Harvard, which also went on to become the first American university to offer graduate studies in Romance languages. Other colleges and universities throughout the United States gradually followed Harvard's example, and today Spanish language and culture may be studied at most American institutions of higher learning.

No discussion of the Spanish influence in the United States, however brief, would be complete without a mention of the Spanish influence on art. Important American artists such as John Singer Sargent, James A. M. Whistler, Thomas Eakins, and Mary Cassatt all explored Spanish subjects and experimented with Spanish techniques. Virtually every serious American artist living today has studied the work of the Spanish masters as well as the great 20th-century Spanish painters Salvador Dalí, Joan Miró, and Pablo Picasso.

The most pervasive Spanish influence in America, however, has probably been in music. Compositions such as Leonard Bernstein's *West Side Story*, the Latinization of William Shakespeare's *Romeo and Juliet* set in New York's Puerto Rican quarter, and Aaron Copland's *Salon Mexico* are two obvious examples. In general, one can hear the influence of Latin rhythms—from tango to mambo, from guaracha to salsa—in virtually every form of American music.

This series of biographies, which Chelsea House has published under the general title HISPANICS OF ACHIEVEMENT, constitutes further recognition of—and a renewed effort to bring forth to the consciousness of America's young people—the contributions that Hispanic people have made not only in the United States but throughout the civilized world. The men and women who are featured in this series have attained a high level of accomplishment in their respective fields of endeavor and have made a permanent mark on American society.

The title of this series must be understood in its broadest possible sense: The term *Hispanics* is intended to include Spaniards, Spanish Americans, and individuals from many countries whose language and culture have either direct or indirect Spanish origins. The names of many of the people included in this series will be immediately familiar; others will be less recognizable. All, however, have attained recognition within their own countries, and often their fame has transcended their borders.

The series HISPANICS OF ACHIEVEMENT thus addresses the attainments and struggles of Hispanic people in the United States and seeks to tell the stories of individuals whose personal and professional lives in some way reflect the larger Hispanic experience. These stories are exemplary of what human beings can accomplish, often against daunting odds and by extraordinary personal sacrifice, where there is conviction and determination. Fray Junípero Serra, the 18th-century Spanish Franciscan missionary, is one such individual. Although in very poor health, he devoted the last 15 years of his life to the foundation of missions throughout California—then a mostly unsettled expanse of land—in an effort to bring a better life to Native Americans through the cultivation of crafts and animal husbandry. An example from recent times, the Mexican-American labor leader Cesar Chavez battled bitter opposition and made untold personal sacrifices in his effort to help poor agricultural workers who have been exploited for decades on farms throughout the Southwest.

The talent with which each one of these men and women may have been endowed required dedication and hard work to develop and become fully realized. Many of them have enjoyed rewards for their efforts during their own lifetime, whereas others have died poor and unrecognized. For some it took a long time to achieve their goals, for others success came at an early age, and for still others the struggle continues. All of them, however, stand out as people whose lives have made a difference, whose achievements we need to recognize today and should continue to honor in the future.

Juan Ponce de León

FIRST CITIZEN
OF A NEW WORLD

Today, his name is all but forgotten, and his deeds are shrouded in the covering mists of history. When the farsighted sailors and determined soldiers who came from Europe to discover, conquer, and settle the Americas are remembered, he is rarely among them. When his name is mentioned, it is as a synonym for folly, for man's eternal gullibility. Lost are the energy, the force of will, and the courage that he shared with his fellow conquistadores, as well as the practicality and commitment that made him special. Instead, Juan Ponce de León, whom poets of the time celebrated as a "manly man whose name was Lion," is mostly remembered today, when he is remembered at all, as a deluded, vainglorious old fool, a maritime Don Quixote hell-bent on a dupe's errand. While his brave and terrible countrymen were claiming treasures and marvelous new lands for themselves and their rulers, credible Ponce de León was sailing endlessly this way and that among the myriad islands of the Caribbean, gulled by his own vanity and the tall tales told by clever Indians into a fruitless search for a so-called fountain of youth: a miraculous spring that would restore youthful vigor to his withered frame once he bathed in or drank from it. Inevitably, his very search brought about that which he so desperately sought to avoid. In the new land known as Florida, not yet visited by the Spanish, the Indians were not so wel-

Juan Ponce de León first became interested in the New World when he witnessed the triumphant return of Christopher Columbus to Spain in 1493. Later that year, he joined Columbus's second expedition to the island of Hispaniola, which today comprises the nations of Haiti and the Dominican Republic.

15

coming. Whatever wonders their land possessed, they were not about to share them with newcomers, and they attacked Ponce de León and his company almost as soon as they set foot on shore.

This image is as mythical as the celebrated fountain of youth itself, for which loyal Ponce de León searched not so much for himself, perhaps, as for his king. Indeed, the entire Spanish adventure in the New World might be seen as a kind of search for a reinvigorating cure: an ailing land, exhausted by years of warfare and division, unable to compete with more robust neighbors, dispatches its mariners in search of the rare and valuable substances (spices and gold) that will restore it to health. The most famous of the Spanish conquistadores, Hernán Cortés, the conqueror of the fabulous Aztec empire of Mexico, made it clear that he was inspired by the need to find a cure for what ailed him. "We Spanish suffer from a disease of the heart which can be cured only by gold," he once wrote. On another occasion he suggested that immortality was, in fact, the prize that he and his conquistadores were pursuing. "The lust for glory extends beyond this mortal life," said Cortés, "and taking a whole world will hardly satisfy it, much less one or two kingdoms."

Such ailments and desires led, in the very last years of the 15th century and the first decades of the 16th century, to one of the most dramatic epochs in all of human history. In 1492, an obscure but fanatically single-minded sailor and mapmaker named Christopher Columbus was given the go-ahead by King Ferdinand and Queen Isabella of Spain to sail west from that country to mysterious Cathay (China) and establish a new trade route that would enable Spain to claim a share of the commerce in spices and other Asian goods that had brought wealth and influence to Spain's Iberian rival, Portugal, and Mediterranean powers such as Venice. Few thought Columbus would succeed, however. He had made such a pest of himself that the monarchs had finally given in to his badgering and agreed to finance his mission, but all knowledge-able observers agreed that the distance westward to Asia across the Ocean Sea, as the Atlantic Ocean was then often called, was far too great for Columbus or anyone else to successfully traverse in the sailing ships of the day. (The notion that the monarchs' advisers opposed Columbus's scheme because they believed the earth to be flat is a myth. The educated men to whom the king and queen turned for advice knew that the earth was round and that theoretically one could therefore reach the Far East by sailing west. The wise men's objection to Columbus's plan was its im-possibility in practice, not in theory. The distances involved were simply too great, they said: on this point they were correct and Columbus was wrong.)

The Spanish conquistador Hernán Cortés, who in 1521 conquered the Aztec empire of Mexico with a force of 600 adventurers. The wealth of Mexico's gold and silver mines soon made Spain one of the world's great powers.

When Columbus returned to Spain in 1493 with the news that he had made landfall on some outlying islands of the Indies, as the spice-producing regions of Asia were indistinctly known to Europeans, the astonishment and acclaim that followed this momentous discovery cannot be overestimated. It was as if today some otherwise undistinguished aviator were to land his propellor plane at a local airport with the news that he or she had flown that relatively primitive vehicle above the earth's atmosphere and landed on the moon. The subsequent revelation, following later voyages by Columbus and other Spanish mariners, that the islands he had discovered were in fact previously unknown lands and the gateway to two "new" continents, populated by unseen peoples and animals and rich in every manner of resource, did not lessen the magnitude of his discovery at all, but in fact enhanced it. The same reaction would occur if today's recreational pilot was revealed to have been mistaken in his or her reports of landing on the moon but had instead reached an unknown nearby planet, one that was occupied by strange but nevertheless recognizably human inhabitants, a plethora of incredible new species of animals and plantlife, and a variety of valuable resources in short supply back on Earth.

There is little doubt that such a discovery would, in many obvious and unforeseen ways, forever change the course of human history, for better or for worse. For the people of his time, Columbus's discovery was no less remarkable. Indeed, as was immediately said, he appeared to have found a whole "new world." Some 500 years from now, the name of the plucky aviator who, from whatever combination of happenstance and vision, discovered the "New Earth" might be as well known as Columbus's. But how would he be judged if the history of the New Earth following its discovery, conquest, and inhabitation by the Old

A map of the world, as conceived by a 12th-century geographer. At this time, Europeans were familiar with the lands bordering the Mediterranean Sea, but they had only a vague idea of the world beyond.

Earthlings paralleled that of the New World following its discovery, conquest, and inhabitation by Europeans? What if the Old Earthlings founded new countries and societies, earned tremendous fortunes, brought new religions and cultural practices, made all manner of scientific and political and cultural innovations, and made of New Earth a world much like our own, with all its wondrous possibilities—but were able to build this new civilization only by destroying the societies of the planet's native inhabitants, making them nearly extinct in the process? What if the Old Earthlings made war on the natives of New Earth for the purpose of their dispersal or removal; if they enslaved them for labor or drove them off their land; or killed them incidentally in even greater numbers, through the most casual contact, by unintentionally transmitting to them germs and viruses for which the natives had no natural immunity? Would our pilot then be celebrated as a prophet or messenger, an

advance scout for civilization, bringing progress, reli-
gion, science, and culture to the "savage" inhabitants
and lands of the newly discovered planet? Or would
he be reviled as a killer, an agent of economic exploitation and cultural genocide who came to conquer
and destroy, who had to eliminate one world in order
to create his own?

And what of those who followed our pilot to the
New Earth, out of restlessness or necessity, to make a
fortune or fulfill their need for adventure, to cure their
"disease of the heart" or their "lust for glory," as stout
Cortés put it, or simply to build a life for themselves
or exercise opportunities and avail themselves of free-
doms denied them in their homeland? What of all
those anonymous individuals who came not to kill or
destroy but simply to live, but whose presence in large
numbers contributed inexorably to the demise of the
New Earthlings? Should these individuals, be they
celebrated or anonymous, be called pioneers, adventurers, explorers, founders, and heroes, or marauders,
conquerors, thieves, usurpers, and murderers? Both?
Or simply earthlings, that is to say, human, with all the
lamentable and praiseworthy qualities of their species?
Such, of course, are the historical judgments still being
made about Columbus, the conquistadores who followed him to the New World, and, to a certain extent,
all those responsible for the European settlement of
the Americas, which continues to this day.

Juan Ponce de León was one of the earliest partici-
pants in this immense historical drama. A gentleman
of Spain, he first saw the New World in 1493 as a
member of Columbus's second expedition, which had
returned to the Caribbean for the express purpose of
establishing a self-sufficient Spanish settlement there.
Though (unlike the cases of Columbus and Cortés
and other more celebrated explorers and conquerors
who were Ponce's contemporaries) none of Ponce's

During the 15th and 16th centuries, Portuguese and Spanish shipbuilders perfected the caravel. Fitted with triangular lateen sails, caravels could tack, or sail against the wind, freeing explorers from complete dependence on winds and currents.

writings have survived, and though much less is known about him than about other such worthies, it seems clear that from the beginning the New World exerted a special hold on him. Unlike most of his wellborn colleagues in the New World, who looked upon their time there as an opportunity to extract a fortune that would enable them to return to a life of luxury and ease in Spain, Ponce, once arrived in the Caribbean, seems to have harbored little desire to return "home." For him, the New World—specifically the magnificent island of Puerto Rico, which he conquered for Spain—immediately became home, less a place to exploit and abandon than one in which to settle and live. In this sense, he was truly one of the first European citizens of the Americas. More than many of his contemporaries, he seems to have been concerned less with how to make a fortune from these new lands (though he was not without material concerns and he certainly made himself wealthy) than with the problems of what it would take for him and his children to live in this New World that Columbus had found. The degree to which he is to be lionized or condemned for the solutions he found to these problems depends largely on how one looks upon the entire great saga of the European settlement of the Americas.

And what of the fountain of youth, that quixotic quest in which Ponce de León met his doom? Consider once again the proposition that a pilot discovers, in our time, a new planet nearby, one easily reached by existing modes of transportation, one recognizably earthlike in essentials such as its environment and atmosphere, but blessed nonetheless with facets of topography and geology, types of plants and vegetation, and varieties of wildlife that are so bewilderingly new to the denizens of Old Earth that they have difficulty even finding language with which to describe them. Such was the experience of the Spanish explorers of the New World, who often found themselves, for example, having to describe such exotic New World specimens as the llama or the buffalo in terms of the cattle, horses, deer, and other animals familiar to those who had never left Spain. Columbus himself was so overcome by the abundance and fertility of the New World that in his letters to Ferdinand and Isabella he often simply gave up trying to provide description, resorting instead to the frequent use of phrases such as, "It must be seen to be believed." This is not simply an ancient phenomenon: as late as the 19th century, many easterners found it impossible to believe the accounts of the geography and the human and animal inhabitants of the American West provided by its explorers.

If, under such circumstances, the discovery of New Earth was followed by reports from its native inhabitants that a plant or tree in one of its deepest, most remote forests contained a substance that could cure

Ponce de León receives a goblet of water from the so-called fountain of youth, for which he searched in vain during his last years in the New World.

cancer or AIDS or some such scourge of modern humanity, how would that report be treated? Perhaps it would be considered fanciful, or even preposterous. But it would not be any more preposterous than the notion that an unknown planet existed within an airplane flight of Earth. It would not be any more preposterous than the idea, during the late 15th century, that two huge unknown continents lay only a little more than one month's voyage to the west of Europe.

And if one of the new settlers of New Earth set off in search of the life-giving elixir, how would he or she be judged almost 500 years from now? As a clown or a dupe? Perhaps. But would not the immense potential benefit of such a substance justify the search? Would not the immense riches that its discoverer would earn justify some risk? And what if he or she found it?

PIUS VLTRA

Si tegat imperium terraque coerceat omnes,
epius explicitatib 3 epiu 3. ver. 61

MAR
PACIFICI AMERI

AN INTERESTING AGE

Hard facts about the life of Juan Ponce de León are as precious and rare as the gold nuggets he searched for in the streams and mines of the New World. Neither the year of his birth, his birthplace, nor the name of his parents, nor the identity of any siblings he might have had is known with certainty. What is known for certain is that he could not have been born into a more fascinating and tumultuous age.

Ponce's birthdate is most often given as 1460, but this contradicts the most authoritative statement on the subject, his own words. According to legal testimony he gave in a court proceeding in Spain in September 1514, he was at that time about 40 years old, which would place his birthdate in approximately 1474. No good reason has been advanced as to why he would have lied about such a matter, so 1474 seems a more likely estimate. It should be mentioned, however, that one source asserts that in a 1519 lawsuit Ponce testified that he was 50 years old. Unlike his earlier testimony, no documentation of this alleged later statement has been presented. Even if one concedes that Ponce testified to this effect in 1519, his statement still places his birthdate closer to 1474 than 1460. Given Ponce's uncertain parentage, it is entirely possi-

A 16th-century engraving celebrating Spain's conquests in the New World; King Ferdinand is depicted at the upper left.

ble that he himself did not know exactly when he had been born, which might account for the discrepancy in his statements.

The date of Ponce's birth is not of tremendous import except—as argued, for example, by Anthony Q. Devereux, author of the sole full-length English-language biography of Ponce de León—as it might relate to the motivation behind his search for the fountain of youth. In 1511, when he and King Ferdinand apparently began laying plans for an expedition to search for the fountain, was Ponce de León still a relatively young man of less than 40, or a middle-aged man past his prime, fast approaching old age by the standards of the day? A definitive answer to that question, which his date of birth would obviously do much to establish, might well determine who was more interested in discovering the restorative fountain, Ponce or his king.

Even less is known of his ancestry. His birthplace is invariably given as San Tervás de Campos, a small town on the Valderaduey River, not far from the city of Valladolid, in the north-central region of Castile and León. His lineage is generally traced to one Count Juan Ponce de León, a Castilian noble who was awarded the title marquis of Cádiz by a grateful King Enrique IV of Castile for his service in reclaiming Cádiz (a port on Spain's southern coast) from a rival for the throne. Among his other accomplishments, the count was the father of at least 21 children out of wedlock. Perhaps the most illustrious of these was Rodrigo Ponce de León, who was Ferdinand and Isabella's most valiant soldier in their war to rid southern Spain of the Moors, North African adherents of Islam who had ruled over much of the country since the 8th century. For his services, the illegitimate Rodrigo was ennobled with the titles of duke of Cádiz and marquis of Zahara.

The explorer Juan Ponce de León's connection to this illustrious family is uncertain, although it is believed that he was a relative. It is speculated that he was either another unknown child of Count Juan Ponce de León or the son, again possibly out of wedlock, of one of the count's many children, but nothing more is known. That he had some connections and prospects and was from a fairly prominent family is indicated by one of the very few facts known about his childhood: according to the 16th-century Spanish historian Fernández de Oviedo, author of one of the first histories of the New World and a personal acquaintance of Ponce, he was sent as a young boy to serve as the page to Pedro Núñez de Guzmán, who was the scion of a leading aristocratic family. As a page, young Ponce would have been expected to act as a kind of personal manservant to Núñez de Guzmán in exchange for an education in all the skills and arts a

The coat of arms of the Ponce family. Little is known for certain about Juan Ponce de León's parents; he may have been the illegitimate son of Count Juan Ponce de León, a leading nobleman in 15th-century Castile.

young nobleman was expected to possess. Ponce would have been taught how to ride a horse, how to conduct himself in combat, and how to hunt with a falcon or hawk. So far as the social graces were concerned, he might have been taught to play backgammon or chess and to play a musical instrument. Núñez de Guzmán would have been expected to find a priest to tutor the boy in the rudiments of Catholicism and possibly to teach him how to read and write, although as Núñez de Guzmán himself was apparently something of a scholar, he might have taken on those responsibilities himself.

Once Ponce reached adolescence, around the age of 14 or 15, his training would have intensified. Now, as his master's squire, he would be responsible not just for helping him dress, taking care of his clothes, and waiting on him at table but also for leading his warhorse into battle, if necessary, and for holding it when the fighting was on foot. His training in the various martial arts—swordplay and jousting—would have become paramount, and he might have been entrusted with delivering important messages across the countryside or with carrying the valuables when his master traveled.

Such an opportunity as Ponce received in the household of Núñez de Guzmán was available only to the sons of the nobility. Fearful that their male children might be spoiled or insufficiently toughened if raised at home, Spain's nobles mutually obliged one another by educating the children of their peers and placing their own likewise with another family. Although Oviedo stated that Núñez de Guzmán was a not very wealthy knight during the time that Ponce spent with him, his true prestige is better indicated by the fact that he was later asked to provide the same tutorial services for Ferdinand, grandson of King Ferdinand and the younger brother of King Charles I of

Knights jousting during a medieval tournament. As a teenager, Ponce undertook the duties of a squire, learning the art of combat and preparing for the day when he would become a knight.

Spain, who as Charles V was also Holy Roman Emperor. Despite his presumably noble birth, Ponce was also described by Oviedo as being a "poor knight," lending credence to the supposition that he was a younger son, with little prospect of inheritance, a fact that might later explain why he decided to seek his fortune in the New World.

Although it is not known for certain, it is generally believed that in the late 1480s Ponce joined Ferdinand and Isabella's campaign to capture Granada, the beautiful ancient city in the region of Andalusia that was the last stronghold of the Moors on the Iberian Peninsula. What exact role he played in the fighting remains unknown, however. If one accepts 1474 or thereabouts as his date of birth, he most likely served Núñez de Guzmán or another knight in the campaign as his squire, which is the role an adolescent nobleman would have been expected to play. A birthdate as early as 1460 would suggest that Ponce, who would then have been approaching 30 years of age, took full part in the action as a mature man of arms. The great hero of Ferdinand and Isabella's victorious siege was Rodrigo Ponce de León, but whether any of his glory was reflected on his presumed kinsman (nephew, most likely) is uncertain.

If Ponce was present for the actual fall of Granada, in early 1492, then his presence would have coincided with that of another man of destiny, an obscure Genoan sailor named Christopher Columbus. For almost a decade, this itinerant mariner had been traveling around western Europe, seeking to convince some king, queen, or nobleman to listen to his proposal to sail west across the Atlantic to the mysterious lands of the Orient, fabled in Europe as lands of unimaginable wealth ever since the return of the 13th-century Venetian traveler Marco Polo. Columbus had received several hearings in the royal courts of Portugal and Spain, and his loyal brother Bartholomew had visited France and England as well in search of backing, but most of those who heard Columbus's scheme were quickly convinced that it was little short of mad.

Citing a hodgepodge of authorities—Old Testament prophets, ancient Greek philosophers, almost-forgotten Arab geographers, Florentine polymaths, Islamic cartographers, Levantine merchants, Jewish wise men, and Marco Polo himself—Columbus sought to persuade anyone who would listen that it was possible to cross the Ocean Sea to Asia. Although every oceangoing power in Europe was interested in developing a direct sea trade route with the Far East, Columbus found it very difficult to interest anyone in his plan.

This lack of interest had nothing to do with misconceptions about the shape of the earth; most educated people in Europe, and anyone who had captained a ship for any significant distance, knew that the earth was round. The problem was that Columbus's numbers, for anyone who made a study of the matter, simply did not add up.

As a young mariner, Christopher Columbus insisted that it was possible to reach Asia by sailing west across the Ocean Sea, now known as the Atlantic Ocean.

In the absence of any knowledge on the part of Europeans of the existence of the continents of North or South America (widespread knowledge of earlier trips to the Americas by Viking explorers had been lost in the intervening centuries) the prevailing worldview held Europe and Asia to be separated by a vast expanse of water often referred to as the Ocean Sea. Theoretically, as Columbus insisted again and again, if one sailed due west across this sea at a given latitude, such as those given by Polo for Cathay and Cipangu (as he called the island nation of Japan, which he had heard about but never visited), one would eventually hit Asian land.

Agreed, said the various experts—monks, physicians, astronomers, mapmakers—to whom Ferdinand and Isabella and King João II of Portugal referred Columbus, but only in theory. All available evidence indicated that the Ocean Sea was simply too wide to be crossed successfully. At the time, European ship's captains seldom sailed out of reach of land for more than several days at a time, in order to make reprovisioning easier, if for no other reason. Now Columbus was proposing to set off directly into the unknown on a voyage that would take months, if not years, to complete.

But it is impossible to reason with a fanatic, and on the matter of his self-styled Enterprise of the Indies the prematurely white-haired Columbus had become fanatical. Seizing upon every obscure snippet of information that could be used to buttress his contentions, willfully misconstruing various references made by the learned men of the ages, indulging in speculative mathematical miscalculations, finding divine support in assorted murky biblical passages, Columbus convinced himself that the distance across the Ocean Sea was but a fraction of its actual extent and could be sailed in a matter of weeks. (By Columbus's calculation, the distance from the Canary Islands, where he would take on his last supplies, to Cipangu was about 2,400 nautical miles. The actual distance, if the Americas were not in the way—a happenstance for which he cannot be blamed—is closer to 11,000 nautical miles.) If he should turn out to be wrong, he explained to those who questioned him, he would stop at certain islands that myth and legend had placed in some undisclosed location in that vast ocean. Besides, he invariably felt compelled to add—and it was not the smallest part of his argument—God had chosen him to carry out this particular mission.

Absolute self-confidence can be extremely persuasive, but few who heard Columbus had been swayed by his arguments. King João of Portugal, according to one of the court historians, "observed this Christopher Columbus to be a big talker and boastful . . . and full of fancy and imagination with his isle Cipangu," so he "gave him small credit." Rejected in Portugal, he tried Spain, where the monarchs referred him to a committee of experts—theologians, lawyers, astronomers, cosmographers—headed by Hernándo de Talavera, the queen's confessor. (Although Catholic dogma, with its frequent insistence on the literal truth of the Bible, did much in the Middle Ages to stymie any increase in geographic knowledge, priests were still often among the most educated men of the age.) The Talavera Commission stalled Columbus for almost five years. In the interim he tried Portugal again, where he was rejected once more. Finally, in the last days of 1490, the Talavera Commission issued to Ferdinand and Isabella its report on the Enterprise of the Indies. Its scathing verdict all but called Columbus a crackpot. "We can find no justification," the learned gentlemen wrote, "for Their Highnesses supporting a project that rests on extremely weak foundations and appears impossible to translate into reality to any person with any knowledge, however modest, of these questions." The king and queen seemed inclined to abide by this assessment.

But in the Christmas season of 1491 the monarchs summoned Columbus to their presence once again, this time at Santa Fe, the fortified camp where they were overseeing the siege of Granada. From their very first meeting, Isabella had been sympathetic toward Columbus, perhaps because the fervor of her own Catholicism matched his own. Now, as if she were

actually contemplating backing his enterprise, she asked him what he would require in terms of personal reward should she and her husband fund his expedition. Incredibly, this foreigner, this commoner, this obscure mariner with virtually nothing in the way of personal achievements to commend him—such as victories in battle or command of earlier expeditions—responded with a list of unprecedented demands. He wanted to be raised to the nobility, with the title Admiral of the Ocean Sea. He wanted to be made viceroy and governor general over any lands that he might discover or conquer in the course of his voyage. He would receive an untaxed 10 percent share in any trade conducted between Spain and the lands

Columbus at the court of King Ferdinand and Queen Isabella. The royal advisers argued that Columbus could not possibly reach Asia with the ships available at the time. They were right, but Columbus's discovery of the Americas more than made up for his misjudgment.

he reached. And after his death these titles, powers, and privileges would pass, in perpetuity, to his sons and succeeding heirs.

Outraged, the monarchs quickly sent him packing. Having wasted his last, best opportunity, Columbus mounted his horse (which the queen had earlier given the impoverished would-be explorer the money to purchase) and rode slowly away from Santa Fe. He was well on his way to La Rábida, the monastery outside the port city of Palos where he had left his son Diego (Columbus was a widower) in the care of the Franciscan friars, when he was overtaken by a royal messenger. The monarchs had agreed to his terms; he was asked to return to Santa Fe to formally conclude negotiations.

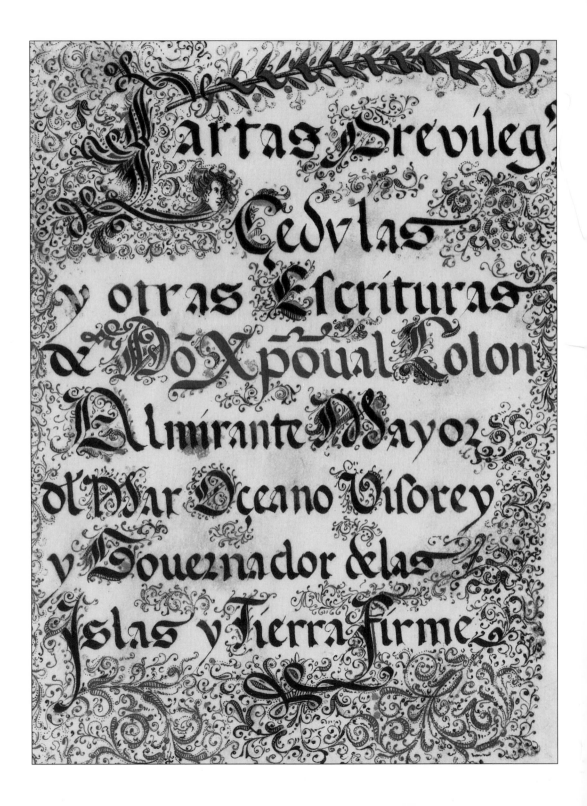

Cartas, Previleg[ios]
Cedulas
y otras Escrituras
d Dō Xpoual Colon
Almirante Mayor
dl Mar Oceano Visorey
y Gouernador delas
Islas y Tierra Firme

C H A P T E R

T H R E E

TO THE NEW WORLD

W hat had happened to make Columbus's seem-ingly outlandish scheme a reality? His calcula-tions were misguided, his arguments farfetched, his demands outrageous. But as circumstances had changed, so had the outlook of the monarchs, particu-larly that of farsighted Isabella. The fall of Granada meant the end of the Moorish presence in Spain and left that country essentially united under Ferdinand and Isabella's rule. The Moorish wars had been drain-ing the country's energy and treasury for centuries; now the Catholic monarchs, as Ferdinand and Isabella were hailed in the wake of their victory over the Muslim infidels, could turn their attention elsewhere. Confident and ambitious, they now sought to solidify and increase their own and their kingdom's power.

The way to do so was through trade, and Spain had a fine example in its neighbor on the Iberian Penin-sula, Portugal. For centuries, the Mediterranean Sea had been the commercial lifeline of Europe. Even its name indicated the centrality of its position in the European worldview. Translated literally, Mediterra-nean means "middle of the land," and for Europeans of the day it was just that: the watery center of the known world, surrounded by the three landmasses of Europe (to the north), mysterious Africa (to the south), and remote and largely unknown Asia (to the east). Those European states that were the richest and most advanced, such as the Italian city-state of Venice,

A page from the Capitulations, the set of privileges and concessions granted to Columbus by Ferdinand and Isabella if he should succeed in reaching the Far East.

Venice, Italy, in the 15th century. At this time, Venice and the other port cities of Italy controlled the Mediterranean Sea and monopolized trade with the East. Spain, Portugal, England, and the Netherlands sought to break this monopoly by finding new sea routes to the riches of Asia.

were those that controlled the largest parts of the sea trade on the Mediterranean, especially the commerce in precious commodities from Asia, which reached the Mediterranean in the Levant (the countries of the Balkan Peninsula and the Middle East that border the Mediterranean, including the present-day nations of Greece, Turkey, Syria, Lebanon, Israel, and Egypt) via various overseas and land trade routes.

Of all the countries of southern Europe, Portugal was at the farthest remove from this crucial trade. Unlike Spain, Portugal did not even have a Mediterranean seaport; virtually all its coastline faced west toward the Atlantic. Isolated overland from the rest of the continent by rugged mountain ranges, possessing little in the way of natural resources, cut off from trade in the Mediterranean, this tiny nation had in the 15th century become Europe's farthest-ranging sea

power, taking the lead in the exploration of new sea routes and in the exploitation of the new lands to which they led.

Much of the exploration was motivated by economics, of course. Europeans desired to reach Asia in order to exploit the trade in such alluring Eastern wares as silk, jade, gems, and especially spices, the most valuable commodity to be had from the East. To Europeans of Ponce de León's time, a "spice" was any of the hundreds of products that were culled or made from exotic, non-European plants: sugar, dyes, perfumes, coffee and tea, cosmetics, drugs, medicines, scented woods such as sandalwood, gums or resins (such as the incense that was used in religious ceremonies), waxes, and even glue.

But the true spices—pepper, nutmeg, mace, cinnamon, and cloves—were the most prized of all. By the

14th century these had become enormously popular in Europe, where, because farmers could seldom produce enough hay or oats to feed their livestock through the long northern winters, most domestic animals raised for food had to be slaughtered each fall. The meat was then smoked or pickled. Pepper and other seasonings helped preserve the meat and also greatly improved its taste and that of other foods as well. Europeans craved the taste of spices to such an extent that it became fashionable for the wealthy to sprinkle mixed pepper and sugar on their toast.

Pepper and other spices reached European consumers by way of a long and complicated trade route. They came from what were generally called the Indies—distant Eastern lands that few Europeans had heard of and none had ever seen. Cinnamon came from the island of Ceylon (now Sri Lanka); pepper from India and from Sumatra in present-day Indonesia; nutmeg and mace from the Ambon island group in the Banda Sea, also part of present-day Indonesia; and cloves from the Spice Islands, a handful of tiny islands north of Ambon. The largest of the Spice Islands were Tidore and Ternate. These islands were also called the Moluccas, and that name gradually came to be used for all the spice-growing islands of eastern Indonesia between Borneo and New Guinea.

In large, heavy cargo ships called junks, Chinese and Malayan merchants plied the waters of the Moluccas, buying fragrant bark, berries, and leaves to sell in the port city of Malacca, a great trading center near the southern tip of the Malay Peninsula. The cargoes that reached Malacca through the swarms of pirates that infested the Java Sea fetched good prices from Indian traders, who shipped the spices to Cochin, Calicut, Goa, and other trade ports on the Malabar Coast, as western India was then called. There, Arab merchants loaded their nimble sailing vessels, called dhows, for the next leg of the trade route to Europe. Some shipments traveled across the Arabian Sea and up the Persian Gulf, to be carried by camel to Baghdad and then to markets in Beirut, Damascus, or Constantinople. Some were shipped across the Indian Ocean and up the Red Sea to Suez, then on to Cairo and Alexandria in Egypt.

Eventually, however, all the spices of the East came to the eastern Mediterranean, where for the first time they passed into European hands. Rich and powerful shipping families in the seafaring Italian cities of Venice and Genoa, backed by the great banking houses of central Europe, controlled the eastern Mediterranean and monopolized the spice trade. Venice, in particular, grew rich on the trade; along the Rialto, the street where the big trading companies were located, a bale of spices that had been purchased

The massive Chinese cargo vessels known as junks were an important part of the Far East trade during the 15th century. Junks brought silks and spices to Malaysia; then Indian and Arab merchants transported the goods to Damascus, Constantinople, Cairo, or Alexandria, where Europeans could trade for them.

for one gold ducat in the Moluccas sold for 100 ducats to dealers who then distributed it to consumers all across the Continent, adding to its price every time it changed hands.

All the while, kings and merchants in every European nation coveted the wealth of Venice. During the 15th century they began to dream of bypassing the Venetians and Arabs entirely—that is, of finding a new way to the spice-laden East. By that time, however, land routes were closed to the Christian nations of Europe by the Ottoman Turks, who controlled western Asia, and by the Ming dynasty rulers of China, who refused to allow outsiders into their country. So the Europeans—in particular the Portuguese—took to the sea.

The great Portuguese age of discovery began in 1419 when a prince named Henry was made governor of the Algarve, Portugal's southwesternmost province. According to his contemporary and biographer Gomes Eanes de Zurara, at Henry's birth the stars foretold that "this prince was bound to engage in great and noble conquests, and above all he was bound to attempt the discovery of things which were hidden from other men, and secret." In the Algarve, Prince Henry the Navigator, as he came to be called, devoted himself to the study of geography. He built a small fort near the village of Sagres, on a cliff that thrust out into the Atlantic, and he invited merchants, travelers, and sailors to visit him, eagerly making notes of their recollections of currents, winds, and coastlines. He stocked his observatory with telescopes and filled his library with maps and books—and he became convinced that the Indian Ocean and the lands to the east could be reached by sailing south and then east, around Africa. (Many cosmographers of the day believed that it was not possible to sail south around Africa because the continent's landmass extended southward all the way around the globe to a point where it connected with Asia. The Ocean Sea, which therefore constituted the present-day Atlantic, Pacific, and Indian oceans, was thus believed to be encompassed by the three known continents of Europe, Asia, and Africa.) At Sagres was perfected the use of the quadrant, cross-staff, and compass for navigation, and it was Henry's shipbuilders who developed the swift, maneuverable vessels known as caravels—nimble ships that combined the cargo-carrying capacity of Arab dhows with the agility of Portuguese river vessels. Caravels were to prove perfectly suited to voyages of exploration. Before his death in 1460, Henry outfitted and launched a series of ocean expeditions that pushed the boundaries of the known world ever outward.

Among Prince Henry's navigators was Nuno Tristão, who in three voyages between 1441 and 1446 mapped the western bulge of Africa as far south as the mouth of the Saloum River in present-day Senegal. Henry was profoundly excited when, in 1444, one of his expeditions rounded Cape Verde, the westernmost point of Africa. Beyond Cape Verde, the great bulk of the continent fell away to the east and south, and the prince was certain that his navigators would soon sail around it entirely and emerge into the Indian Ocean. As it turned out, however, Henry had vastly underestimated the size of the African continent, and by the time of his death the farthest point reached by his expeditions was the coast of what is today Sierra Leone.

The Portuguese may still have been far from the Indies, but the potential profit in oceangoing exploration had been demonstrated. In 1444, the same year that one of Henry's ships rounded Cape Verde, another African expedition returned to Portugal with some precious cargo—250 Africans to be sold as slaves. This

demonstration of the profit to be gained from the prince's explorations quieted those who had criticized the voyages as a frivolous quest after the unknowable. In a short time, the names given to the various regions of the coastline "discovered" by Portugal's master mariners in the Gulf of Guinea—Grain Coast, Ivory Coast, Slave Coast, Gold Coast—reflected the source of the wealth that European traders and merchants were extracting from that territory.

After Henry's death, the kings of Portugal contin-ued to send out new expeditions. Each doggedly inched its way southward along the unknown west coast of Africa, battling heat, disease, shoal water, and, occasionally, native inhabitants. In 1473 the Portuguese crossed the equator. In 1483 Diogo Cão passed the mouth of the Congo River. The next year, Columbus made his first pitch for support from Portugal's King João II. But the Portuguese had spent more than half a century pioneering the eastern route around Africa, and João, put off as well by Columbus's arrogance, declined to back his venture.

That decision seemed to be justified when, in 1487–88, João's captain Bartolomeu Dias rounded the southern tip of the Dark Continent (so-called because Europeans possessed so little knowledge of Africa that it usually appeared on maps of the day as a large, indistinct shape with a dark, featureless interior) and entered the Indian Ocean. Though the pleading of his crew convinced Dias to turn around and return to Portugal without reaching India, he had proved that it was indeed possible to sail around Africa and, presumably, thereby reach the Indies. According to some sources, the Columbus brothers were in Lisbon, Portugal's capital city, when Dias's ships returned. They had come to importune João once more about the Enterprise of the Indies, but upon hearing of Dias's achievement they recognized at once that their mission in Portugal was futile.

Almost 10 years later a Portuguese fleet consisting of four ships and led by Vasco da Gama bettered Dias's feat by sailing southward around Africa, then northward along its east coast, finally reaching India, where it acquired a load of spices with which it returned to Lisbon in 1499. Portugal at last had its sea route to the Indies, and in a letter to Ferdinand and Isabella (who had just become his in-laws), Manoel I, Portugal's new king, could not help but gloat: "We learn that they did reach and discover India and other kingdoms and

lordships bordering upon it; that they entered and navigated its seas, finding large cities, large edifices and rivers, and great populations, among whom is carried on all the trade in spices and precious stones."

The consequences of da Gama's voyage were immediate and momentous, finishing a process that Prince Henry the Navigator had begun: Tiny, isolated Portugal had become the leading commercial nation of Europe. By 1503, pepper sold in Lisbon for onefifth of what it cost in Venice, and over the ensuing decades power in Europe would shift from those states that dominated the Mediterranean to those that controlled the oceans.

Da Gama's voyage was still in the future at the time of Columbus's royal audience at Santa Fe, of course, but Portugal's transformation was sufficiently well advanced to indicate to the Catholic monarchs the desirability of developing their own new trade routes. With the 700-year war with the Moors concluded,

Vasco da Gama delivers letters from the king of Portugal to an Eastern potentate. In 1498, da Gama led a fleet of four ships around the southern tip of Africa and reached India. The next year, he returned to Lisbon with the first cargo of spices to be transported back to Europe on European vessels.

Ferdinand and Isabella could now devote some of their country's resources to this project, and Columbus happened to be on hand with a proposal, hare-brained as some found it to be. Admittedly, there was only a very small likelihood of his succeeding, argued Luis Santangel, a wealthy businessman who served as the king's treasurer, but what if he did? The cost of the expedition was, in relative terms, not so very great, and he, Santangel, was willing to raise the needed funds. And should the mad Genoan somehow succeed, Santangel continued, the reward for Spain would be incalculable, and the demands Columbus had made a very small price to pay. So Columbus was called back to Santa Fe, and an agreement with the Crown, called the Capitulations, was reached.

Whether Ponce de León was at Santa Fe in early 1492, when the Capitulations were signed, and

Columbus and his crew give thanks to God upon landing in the New World in 1492.

whether this was the first time he heard of the Enterprise of the Indies, will likely never be known. But
certainly he would have been aware of the extraordinary events of the spring of 1493, when the returned
Columbus made the long overland journey from the
port of Palos to Ferdinand and Isabella's court at
Barcelona.

Derided not long before as a madman, Columbus
had stepped ashore as Spain's grandest hero. Having
been forced to put in at Lisbon for repairs, the letter
he had written Ferdinand and Isabella announcing his
discovery—a number of islands, foremost among
them a magnificent land he named Hispaniola, which
was filled with spices and gold and inhabited by timid,
peace-loving people who could be easily conquered

*The return of Columbus
to the Spanish court at
Barcelona was a triumphal
procession of adventurers
displaying their discoveries
—exotically dressed New
World natives, tropical
animals, and samples of
gold and amber.*

and put to work as slaves—had preceded him to Spain, and his journey to court became a triumphal procession. Peasants and nobles alike turned out to see the exotic cavalcade of bold adventurers, New World natives in plumed headdresses and fishbone-and-gold ornaments, and brightly colored parrots and other birds. Hired servants followed Columbus and his officers, bearing items of pure gold and amber. In the courtyard of the royal palace in Barcelona, the nobility rose as one when Columbus entered, an honor usually reserved only for the sons of the land's most important families. In the palace's great hall, where Columbus knelt at the feet of Ferdinand and Isabella, the monarchs made him rise and sit at the queen's right hand while he described his adventures. At dinner with the monarchs that evening, Columbus was served in a manner known as *salva*—that is, with a cover over his plate, which was brought out after the king had tasted his food. This high honor was usually reserved for persons of royal blood.

After the toasting and celebrating were concluded, Ferdinand and Isabella let it be known that Columbus was to waste no time in organizing a return expedition to colonize the lands he had found. This accorded with his own wishes. Whereas for the first voyage he had been forced to accept convicts in order to man his vessels, this time he was deluged by volunteers eager to make their fortune on Hispaniola. Among them, as a foot soldier, was a young knight—"somewhat of ruddy hue, with a pleasing face, affable," according to one of the few surviving contemporary descriptions of him—named Ponce de León.

Conquering Hispaniola

As with virtually all of the known events of Juan Ponce de León's life, one can only surmise, rather than state with absolute certainty, certain things about his decision to voyage to the New World, as Columbus's discovery came to be called. Most obviously, the decision suggests that he had a shortage of prospects in Spain, as well as a restless and adventurous temperament.

That Ponce occupied something less than an exalted social status in Spain is indicated by the almost complete lack of any documentary evidence—land deeds, inheritance records, birth or baptismal records, military accounts, legal papers—linking him to his homeland before he emerges in the historical record on the New World island of Hispaniola. That he was footloose or ambitious, as well as obscure, is demonstrated by the very fact of his emigration at such an early date in Spain's history in the Americas. Though Columbus had no trouble finding volunteers for his second voyage, in all likelihood very few of these were contented or settled in their homeland. There was simply little reason for anyone who was well established in Spain to risk a new beginning on Hispaniola. To be sure, several hundred hidalgos accompanied Columbus on his second voyage, but these members of the lesser nobility were most likely at loose ends in

The caravel was a small, swift vessel with a substantial cargo capacity, and it was the ideal ship of the time for exploration and for transporting back to Europe the wealth of the Americas. The caravels in this painting are the ships of Columbus: the Niña, Pinta, *and* Santa María.

Spain, being younger sons with little prospect of inheritance, possibly from families left impoverished by the Moorish wars. Indeed, the conclusion of the wars was itself a spur to emigration, for the sons of the nobility were trained at arms, and peace left many of them yearning for a new adventure. In general, it may safely be said that the chief attraction for those who did decide to make their way in the New World was the prospect of living in a way they never could at home: that is, as lords, with Indian slaves to extract for them an amount of gold—which Columbus promised existed in abundance on Hispaniola—sufficient for them to return to Spain in splendor and live out the remainder of their days in luxury.

Whether this or something like it was young Ponce's ambition is unknown. That he was a member of the second Columbus expedition is generally accepted, although his name has never been discovered

An 18th-century map of Hispaniola. Columbus hoped to derive great wealth from the island, but the poor discipline of the Spanish settlers and the resistance of the Indians caused him no end of trouble.

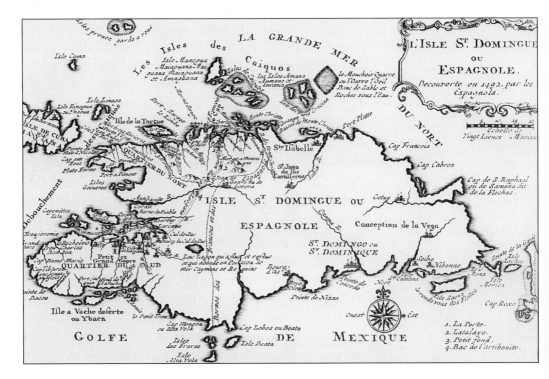

on any of the expedition's membership rolls. The source for the belief that Ponce de León first came to the New World at this time is Bartolomé de Las Casas, who in 1510 would become the first Catholic priest ordained in the Americas. Las Casas, who would subsequently win fame as the so-called Apostle to the Indies, was also one of the first historians of Spain's conquest of the New World.

According to Las Casas, Ponce sailed with Columbus not as one of the "gentlemen of the land," as the higher-born members of the expedition were known—those who could expect, in Hispaniola, to be granted a large number of Indians who would perform for them, in virtual slavery, the hard work of clearing land, growing food, and mining gold—but as a common foot soldier. As such, he would have been expected, along with the expedition's other soldiers, to press Hispaniola's native inhabitants into subjugation.

That task, according to Columbus, would not be a difficult one. From the moment, in December 1492, of his first encounter with the natives of Hispaniola (a large semitropical island in the Caribbean—southeast of the state of Florida, between the much smaller islands of Jamaica and Puerto Rico and southeast of the large island of Cuba—home today to the nations of Haiti and the Dominican Republic), Columbus had been impressed by their generosity and their apparently peaceful and gentle nature. This made them perfectly suited, he immediately concluded, to become the Spaniards' slaves.

"They are so artless and free with all they possess," he wrote in the shipboard letter he composed for Ferdinand and Isabella, "that no one would believe it without having seen it. Of anything they have, if you ask them for it, they never say no; rather they invite the person to share it, and show as much love as if they were giving their hearts; and whether the thing be of value or of small price, at once they are content with whatever little thing of whatever kind may be given to them." They are "wonderfully timorous," he continued, unwilling to use weapons because they are "timid beyond cure." In his private log, where he was free of the need to impress Ferdinand and Isabella of the wonderful qualities of every aspect of his discovery, he used harsher terms. There, he wrote that the Indians (a term that Columbus first used for them because he still believed that he had reached the Indies) were not timid or gentle but "very cowardly."

But whether speaking to his rulers by letter or to himself in his ship's journal, Columbus reached a clear conclusion about the native inhabitants of Hispaniola. "With 50 armed men these people could be brought under control and made to do whatever one might wish," he informed the Catholic monarchs. The Indians were "fit to be ordered about and made to work, to sow and do [whatever] else that may be needed," he confided to his log. "To rule here, one need only get settled and assert authority over the natives, who will carry out whatever they are ordered to do. I, with my crew—barely a handful of men—could conquer all these islands with no resistance whatsoever. The Indians always run away; they have no arms, nor the warring spirit. They are naked and defenseless, hence ready to be given orders and put to work."

Columbus's second expedition, with its 1,200 men and 17 ships, was his first attempt to implement his plan to "get settled and assert authority over the natives." In addition to several hundred hidalgos, a body of foot soldiers, and the crews necessary to sail the ships, Columbus brought with him an undisclosed number of individuals listed as "farmers" (that is, peasants or members of the class accustomed to actually working, rather than owning, the land); a cavalry

Columbus on the deck of his flagship. The Admiral of the Ocean Sea's second voyage to the Americas consisted of 17 ships and 1,200 men, whose number included Ponce de León.

troop, also for use in subjugating the Indians; six priests to convert them to Catholicism; several fierce dogs, probably greyhounds, to keep them terrified; and a supply of horses, pigs, sheep, and grain, as well as feed for various animals.

Though it has often been stated that the purpose of Columbus's second voyage was to establish a permanent settlement on Hispaniola, there is some indication that a more likely goal was simply to found what essentially amounted to a trading outpost and supporting colony, manned by a shifting population. Establishment of a permanent settlement would require, besides agricultural self-sufficiency, the presence of women as a means of repopulation. Men intending to stay in the New World brought women with them. The job of this first delegation of Spanish was to conquer and build, not necessarily to settle.

If one accepts Las Casas's statement that Ponce de León was a member of Columbus's second voyage, then it seems clear that he participated in some significant way in the conquest of Hispaniola. A few biographers, seeking to distance Ponce from the bloody events that unfurled on Hispaniola after Columbus's return there in November 1493, assert that he went

back to Spain shortly thereafter and did not revisit the
New World for many years, probably not until 1502,
with the great armada of 30 ships commanded by
Nicolás de Ovando.

As there is, however, no documentary evidence of
his presence in Spain at that time, Las Casas's statement
placing him in the New World seems persuasive.
Moreover, when Ponce does at last appear in the
historical record, he is mentioned as the "captain" of
the "people of war" of Santo Domingo—that is, as the
recognized leader of the Spanish forces from their
settlement of Santo Domingo (now the capital city of
the Dominican Republic) in their war against the
Indians. Given Ponce's demonstrably obscure status in
Spain prior to his sailing with Columbus, and Las
Casas's statement that he was but a poor foot soldier
when he shipped to the New World, it seems most
likely that Ponce had attained the elevated status of
captain with which he reappears in the historical
record by distinguishing himself in battle with his
fellow Spaniards against the native population of Hispaniola sometime prior to 1502.

That Ponce's name is absent for a time from the
chronicle of events on Hispaniola is not necessarily
surprising, for many of the details of what took place
there in the first years of the Spanish presence have
been lost. For the Spanish there was very little to
celebrate, and there are no Indians left to tell the tale.

What is clear is that Columbus's fleet, "so united
and so handsome," according to him, sailed from the
Spanish port of Cádiz on September 25, 1493. It put
in for its final provisions at the Canary Islands on the
second day of October and departed from there for
Hispaniola 10 days later, on the one-year anniversary
of the Admiral of the Ocean Sea's first landfall in the
New World. Fine weather and favorable winds—day
after day the "sun rose on a sea as smooth as polished

marble," wrote the expedition's physician, Diego Alvárez Chanca—brought the fleet to the Caribbean in just three weeks, with Columbus "discovering" and naming such islands of the Lesser Antilles as Dominica, Guadeloupe, Montserrat, Nevis, St. Kitts, and the Virgin Islands as he proceeded northwestward toward his destination. To the east of Hispaniola the fleet sailed along the south coast of a large island, described by Columbus as "very lovely and very fertile," that the Indians of the region called Borinquén. This was presumably Ponce de León's first glimpse of his future home, the island that would come to be known as Puerto Rico.

The first indication that Columbus might have erred in some of his early assessments of Hispaniola came almost immediately. On the first voyage, Columbus's flagship, the *Santa María,* had run aground on a coral reef just after midnight on Christmas Eve, shredding its hull. Using the timbers of the wrecked ship to erect a small fort, 40 Spaniards volunteered to remain behind on Hispaniola, excited by the prospect of carving out huge properties for themselves and growing rich from the gold that the native people of the area seemed to possess in such abundance. Those who stayed behind were provisioned with a year's worth of wine, bread, and grain from the ship's stores and were defended by the ship's guns, and they no doubt shared Columbus's optimism about their prospects. "When I return here from Castile," the Admiral of the Ocean Sea wrote in his journal, "I shall find such riches extracted from this land that the king and queen, within three years' time, will be able to prepare and carry out the reconquest of the Holy Sepulcher in Jerusalem." (That is, Ferdinand and Isabella could use all their newfound New World wealth to fund a new crusade to free the Holy Land from the control of the Ottoman Turks, who were Muslim unbelievers in the eyes of Christian Europe and especially the devoutly Catholic Columbus.) Probably located just to the east of the present-day city of Cap-Haitien in the country of Haiti, this first European settlement in the New World was called Navidad by Columbus, since it was founded on Christmas Day.

It was to Navidad then that Columbus took his second fleet. While they were still some 25 miles to the east he sent ashore a landing party that was to scout for likely sites for further settlement. This group returned quickly to the ships with news of a disturbing discovery: the decomposing corpses of two men. The bodies had been lashed together, and the men appeared to be Spanish. Columbus hurried his fleet to Navidad, where it arrived at nightfall on November 27, 1493. Signal torches were set, and the ships' guns were fired, but there was no response from shore. In the morning the grisly truth was discovered. Navidad was a charred ruin; the corpses of its defenders were found for miles around. There were no survivors.

Columbus soon pieced together the grim truth. Discipline among the Spaniards who had remained behind at Navidad had quickly broken down. They desired gold and women, and the Indians had both. Raiding parties regularly plundered the countryside. Understandably, the Indians soon tired of such behavior; a chieftain named Caonabo organized several

In this engraving, a Caribbean Indian chief informs his people of the arrival of strangers in ships. Columbus described the natives of Hispaniola as docile and cooperative, eager to trade gold nuggets for small trinkets.

highly effective ambushes and then set upon Navidad with a huge war party. The 10 defenders of the fortress who had survived the forays into the interior were easily overrun.

The incident at Navidad did not cause the Spanish to change their behavior toward the Indians at all; if anything, it only encouraged further aggression by appearing to belie Columbus's assertion that the Indians were gentle and nonaggressive. Within four days of the Spanish establishment of a new settlement, Isabela, some 75 miles east of Navidad, an armed band had been sent into the interior to search for gold. It was led by Alonso de Ojeda, who was described by Las Casas as "very devoted to the Virgin Mary but the first to spill blood wherever there was any dispute or conflict."

The description might very well have been extended to virtually all of the Spanish on Hispaniola, who were quick to proclaim their Catholic faith but were seldom willing to behave in a Christian manner toward the Indians. With Columbus proving a spectacularly inefficient administrator, unable to impose any sort of discipline over his men, Spanish raiding parties were soon crisscrossing the interior of the island. Few of the Spanish seemed interested in the hard work of clearing and planting fields, raising buildings, or doing the other tasks necessary to establish a self-sufficient settlement. They had come to the New World to be lords, not peasants, and they resented any attempt by Columbus to impose order upon them. He complained that "the Spaniards which he took with him into these regions were given rather to sleep, play, and idleness rather than to labor." According to his son and biographer Ferdinand, the would-be colonists were men who "had embarked on the voyage with the idea that as soon as they landed they could load themselves with gold and return home

rich" and were thus "disgruntled at having to work on the construction of the new town."

They had energy to seek after gold, however. The unfamiliar climate and food and Isabela's unfortunate location near a malarial swamp left hundreds of the settlers disabled by illness at any given time, but those who ventured into the interior on gold expeditions tended to feel much better. In March 1494 Columbus himself led 500 Spanish into the mountains of the interior, where gold nuggets had been found in some of the streams. Though the Spanish were unsuitably clad and suffered through "20 days with terrible weather, bad food and worse drink," according to Michele de Cuneo, a member of that expedition, "out of covetousness of that gold, we all kept strong and lusty."

An engraving made in 1598 shows Spanish explorers receiving gifts from the Indians. Hernán Cortés, the conqueror of Mexico, once wrote, "We Spanish suffer from a disease of the heart which can be cured only by gold."

For all their goldlust, the Spanish did not intend to mine or pan for the precious metal themselves. That was what, to their way of thinking, the Indians were for. The natives were also most useful for clearing fields and planting and tending crops, other work the Spanish disdained. They could themselves also be converted into a cash commodity as slaves shipped in chains back to Spain.

These people, known as the Taino (from their own word for "good" or "noble"), or island Arawaks, had little means of resisting the Spanish. Despite Caonabo's success with the marauders of Navidad, Columbus's assessment of the Indians was accurate in many respects. The Taino were a pastoral people who had fashioned a remarkably peaceful society. They lived in small villages of 10 to 15 families, the members of which occupied "remarkably clean and tidy" (according to Las Casas) circular houses. The houses were fashioned from cane poles set in the ground "as close as the fingers of a hand" (Columbus's words) and covered by a wood-frame roof overlaid first with tightly woven branches and vines and then with large palm leaves. Overseeing several villages was a hereditary official known as a cacique.

The Taino's remarkably efficient agricultural system had allowed them to prosper on Hispaniola, where they grew manioc root (from which was made cassava bread, the staple of their diet), a form of sweet potato called *batata,* and various squashes and beans in fields of low mounds called *conuco*s.

According to the historian David Watts, "conuco agriculture seems to have provided an exceptionally ecologically well-balanced and protective form of land use." Conucos could be adapted for use in virtually any topographic condition; the root crops, such as manioc, served to prevent erosion and replenish the soil with essential nutrients, while the leaf crops, such as beans, provided shade from the powerful Caribbean sunlight. Combined with the beneficial Caribbean climate, conuco agriculture provided a continuous yearlong harvest that, according to Columbus biographer Kirkpatrick Sale, was "highly productive, surpassing in yields anything known in Europe at the time, with labor that amounted to barely two or three hours a week." In the judgment of the geographer Carl Sauer, a pioneer in the study of pre-Columbian ways of life in the Americas, Taino agriculture was "productive as in few parts of the world," providing the "highest returns of food in continuous supply by the simplest methods and modest labor." This agricultural proficiency, combined with the harmonious ways of their society, had enabled the Taino to flourish: the most responsible modern estimates of their population on Hispaniola at the time of the Spanish arrival place it at 3 million. (Some researchers would set that figure as high as 8 million.)

But 3 million Taino were no match for 1,000 Spanish (the estimated population on Hispaniola in 1502, by which time there is no doubt Ponce de León was present on the island) single-mindedly determined on their subjugation. Inexperienced in warfare, the Taino had nothing to match the Spanish weapons, which included arquebuses (early firearms), crossbows, and metal implements of war such as swords and daggers. The Indians were terrified of the horses the Spanish brought with them from Spain (horses are not native to the New World), as well as by the vicious dogs that the Spanish used to hunt them down.

Most of all the Taino were simply overawed by the cruelty and ferocity the Spanish displayed toward them. In February 1495 Columbus and his men rounded up 1,600 Taino for shipment as slaves to Spain. This was far more than his ships could carry, so only 550—"the best males and females," according to

Cuneo—were taken in chains aboard the vessels. "Of the rest who were left," Cuneo continued, "the announcement went around that whoever wanted them could take as many as he pleased; and this was done. And when everyone had been supplied there was some 400 of them left to whom permission was granted to go wherever they wanted. Among them there were many women who had infants at their breast. They, in order the better to escape us, since they were afraid we would turn to catch them again, left their infants anywhere on the ground and started to flee like desperate people."

Because the heartlessness of such scenes offended the sensibilities of the Catholic monarchs, enslaving the Indians was prohibited on Hispaniola shortly thereafter. Instead, a new system, called the *encomienda,* was instituted. Under this arrangement, the monarch (or his representative, Columbus in this case) could give, or commend, Indians to his subjects, the colonists or *encomenderos.* Theoretically, the encomienda was a system of mutual responsibilities. The Spanish were

A woodcut showing the Spanish conquistadores beating and torturing Indian slaves. The Spanish behaved brutally to any natives who would not labor for them or collect gold. Eventually they would come close to exterminating the natives of Hispaniola, and they would have to import slaves from Africa to work on their plantations.

free to do with the Indians essentially as they liked in terms of forcing labor from them, but the Indians in turn were to be compensated by receiving instruction in Christian doctrine as well as shelter and food. The encomienda was, in short, little more than slavery by another name. On top of this, Columbus soon instituted a system of forced tribute whereby each Indian over the age of 14 was required to produce enough gold every three months to fill a small flask. The penalty for noncompliance was to have one's hands cut off, whereupon most offenders subsequently bled to death.

The island that Columbus had described to his monarchs as a virtual paradise soon became a hell for its inhabitants. Not inclined much to kindness toward the Indians in any event, Columbus quickly grew more concerned with further exploration than with the governance of Hispaniola. His arbitrary and despotic rule when he was present on the island, combined with the similar inefficiency of his brothers Bartholomew and Diego (who acted as his lieutenants in his frequent absences) and the rebellious and willful nature of the settlers, left the island in a state of chaos bordering on anarchy. "Each one went where he willed among the Indians," Ferdinand Columbus later wrote, "stealing their property and wives and inflicting so many injuries upon them that the Indians resolved to avenge themselves.... The Admiral found the island in a pitiful state, with most of the Christians committing innumerable outrages for which they were mortally hated by the Indians, who refused to obey them."

Taino resistance proved futile, however. A huge Taino force gathered in the valley of the Vega Real to oppose Columbus's March 1495 expedition, but the Spaniards' weaponry enabled them to prevail, and the battle turned into a brutal massacre. After that, Taino resistance was sporadic and isolated, taking as its most characteristic form flight into the mountains, where, it was hoped, the Spanish would not pursue them in search of labor and tribute. Acting upon an apparently peaceful entreaty from one of Columbus's lieutenants, the Taino cacique Caonabo was tricked into slavery and shipped in chains to Spain, dying en route. Another influential cacique, Guacanagari, who had been quick to befriend Columbus, was eventually, according to Las Casas, forced to flee "from the massacres and cruelties of the Christians" to the mountains, where "he died a wanderer, deprived of his state." By 1500 the Spanish had established at least seven fortresses across the island, and 340 gallows crossed the Vega Real alone. From these gibbets, miscreant Taino were "hung just high enough for their feet to nearly touch the ground," according to Las Casas. While the slowly suffocating Taino dangled, 13 Spanish at a time (the number had sacred significance: it was the number of those in attendance at the Last Supper—namely, Jesus Christ and his 12 apostles) heaped kindling and wood beneath their feet "and with fire they burned the Indians alive." Even after Columbus was, at Ferdinand and Isabella's orders, replaced as governor of Hispaniola in 1500 and brought back to Spain in chains, the situation on the island did not improve for the Taino.

Las Casas, who arrived on Hispaniola for the first time in 1502 with the Ovando armada and initially took part in the conquest as a soldier, records an almost unimaginable legacy of Spanish brutality. Some measure of Taino resistance apparently continued, for Las Casas writes of his countrymen that "they made a law among themselves that for one Christian whom the Indians killed, the Christians should kill a hundred Indians." Assuring his readers that "I saw all the above things . . . all these did my own eyes witness," he described appalling atrocities. His fellow Spaniards "made bets as to who would slit a [Taino] man in two, or cut off his head at one blow; or they opened up his bowels. They tore the babes from their mother's breast by their feet, and dashed their head against the rocks. . . . They spitted the bodies of other babes, together with their mothers and all who were before them, on their swords."

On another occasion Las Casas was with a group of Spanish soldiers when they came upon a Taino village where the people had gathered in the plaza: "A Spaniard, in whom the devil is thought to have clothed himself, suddenly drew his sword. Then the whole hundred drew theirs and began to rip open the bellies, to cut and kill those lambs—men, women, children, and old folk, all of whom were seated, off

Bartolomé de Las Casas, known as the Apostle to the Indies, was the first Catholic priest ordained in the New World. In his writings, Las Casas condemned the savagery and brutality of his fellow Spaniards as they sought to subdue the natives of the Americas.

guard and frightened, watching the horses and the Spaniards. And within two credos [a measurement of distance], not a man of all of them remains alive. The Spaniards enter the large house nearby, for this was happening at its door, and in the same way, with cuts and stabs, begin to kill as many as they found there, so that a stream of blood was running. . . . To see the wounds which covered the bodies of the dead and dying was a spectacle of horror and dread."

Apologists for the Spanish often try to discredit Las Casas by claiming that his religious fervor caused him, in writing his accounts, to greatly exaggerate Spanish atrocities in the conquest of the New World. Yet many contemporaries corroborate the general import of his accounts. To cite just one example, Fernández de Oviedo, who wrote the first officially commissioned Spanish history of the New World and is generally regarded as a champion of the Spanish presence there, wrote that the fabled "conquistadores [should] more accurately be called depopulators or squanderers of the new lands." Like "veritable hangmen or headsmen or executioners or ministers of Satan," these "soldiers" caused "various innumerable and cruel deaths . . . as uncountable as the stars."

In despair at the destruction of their world, many of the Taino resisted in the last and only way that they had: they killed themselves in large numbers rather than serve the Spanish. According to Las Casas, the most common method of suicide was to drink the juice of the manioc root, which is lethally poisonous if left untreated and uncooked. Pregnant women also began using various herbs to induce abortion rather than bring their children into a world made suddenly so cruel. Others, the majority in all likelihood, simply gave themselves up to the Spanish and their fate: "In this time, the greatest outrages and slaughterings of people were perpetrated, whole villages being depopulated. . . . The Indians saw that without any offense on their part they were despoiled of their kingdoms, their lands and liberties and of their lives, their wives, and homes. As they saw themselves each day perishing by the cruel and inhuman treatment of the Spaniards, crushed to the earth by the horses, cut in pieces by swords, eaten and torn by dogs, many buried alive and suffering all kinds of exquisite tortures, some . . . decided to abandon themselves to their unhappy fate with no further struggles, placing themselves in the hands of their enemies that they might do with them as they liked." So wrote Las Casas.

Even had the Spanish been inclined to treat these despairing souls gently, the mere fact of contact between the two peoples would probably have been sufficient to destroy the peaceful Taino. For along with the livestock (cattle, horses, and pigs) that overran the Indians' fields and destroyed all manner of essential indigenous plant life; the weaponry that subdued them; and the invasive manner of European agriculture that left the island, in Las Casas's word, a "desert" in comparison to the thickly forested land that Columbus had first seen, the Spanish brought something else with them: germs. The various infectious agents that cause such diseases as influenza, measles, typhus, pneumonia, tuberculosis, diphtheria, pleurisy, and especially smallpox were foreign to the Western Hemisphere, whose peoples had therefore developed no protective immunity to them.

Thus the mere presence of the Spanish, in whose bodies these microbes traveled, served unwittingly as the most potent vehicle of "germ warfare" that a military strategist could ever have desired. For all their bloodthirstiness, the Spanish did not wish to exterminate the Indians, but to terrorize them into utter and abject subjugation; they needed the Indians to work for them. European diseases were much more efficient

The Spanish brought to the Americas a number of diseases to which the Indians had no resistance. In this illustration from a Spanish history of the conquest of the New World, the various stages of death from smallpox are shown.

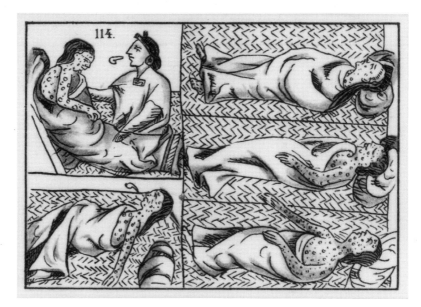

than their carriers, however, and in combination with the other effects of the conquest they brought about a holocaust on Hispaniola, where far more Indians perished from new diseases than from Spanish arms or mistreatment. (The same general pattern of conquest and European-borne disease played itself out with similar consequences virtually everywhere in the New World.) The total numbers are astounding and tragic. By 1514 there were approximately 28,000 Taino left on Hispaniola, from a population that measured from 3 to 8 million just slightly more than two decades earlier, when Columbus first laid eyes on the island. Within three decades more, just 200 Taino remained. Ten years or so later, they were gone, and the island was populated solely by the Spanish, their European competitors (namely the French), and, in a short time, the hundreds of thousands of black Africans the Europeans would import as slaves to replace the eradicated Indian labor force.

F I V E

BORINQUÉN
AND BECERILLO

Though Ponce de León's whereabouts between 1495 and 1502 may be debated, it is established beyond question that by the latter year he was one of several hundred inhabitants of Santo Domingo, the principal Spanish "city" on Hispaniola, which was located on the south shore of the island. There he met, courted, and married his first wife, Leonor, who is said to have been the daughter of an innkeeper in the city. As an innkeeper's daughter, Leonor would not, perhaps, have been considered an especially attractive marriage prospect by the standards of the Spanish nobility back in the homeland. On Hispaniola, however, Ponce was considered to have made a distinguished match simply because his wife was Spanish-born. According to contemporary sources, the dowry he obtained from Leonor's father greatly enhanced his social status in Santo Domingo and helped bring him to the attention of Nicolás de Ovando, the governor of the island. Together, Ponce and Leonor would have four children: (in order of birth) Juana, María, Isabel, and Luis.

But Ponce mostly called attention to himself by his skill in battle, and by 1504 he had been appointed by Ovando to lead Santo Domingo's forces against the still-rebellious natives of the province of Higüey, as the easternmost portion of Hispaniola was known. Angered by the Spaniards' insistent demands for cassava bread, gold, and women, the Indians of Higüey had

A contemporary Spanish postage stamp depicting Ponce de León. By the early 1500s, Ponce was a prominent citizen of Santo Domingo, the capital of Hispaniola.

71

overrun and burned the sole Spanish fortress, killing 9 of the 10 members of its small garrison. The sole survivor made his way to Santo Domingo with his sad tale, and Ovando organized a retaliatory campaign with forces from the primary Spanish settlements—Santo Domingo, Santiago, La Vega, and Boana, approximately 300 men in all—supplemented by Indians pressed into service from the more quiescent province of Ycayagua.

Details of the Higüey campaign are scarce, but Ponce apparently distinguished himself in combat, for in its aftermath he was named by Ovando to act as his deputy governor in that province. The Indians there had proved as ill-equipped as the natives of the rest of the island to resist the Spanish. Las Casas describes a typical encounter in which a small detachment of Spanish soldiers, perhaps 10 or 12 men, was waylaid by a large contingent of Taino warriors that modern historians have numbered at several hundred. Hurling rocks and firing arrows tipped with stone, the Indians were able to keep the Spanish at bay for several hours, but the Spaniards' armor and shields protected them from serious injury. Meanwhile, fear of the Spanish crossbows kept the Indians from venturing into close enough range to wield their wooden clubs—called *macanas*—to any great effect, while those who did stray too near found themselves overmatched by the Spaniards' metal swords. In time the Spanish battalion was rescued by a larger delegation, and with a lesser disparity in numbers the superiority of the Spanish weaponry was even more telling.

So it went throughout the campaign, with the technological advantage enjoyed by the Spanish more than offsetting the Indians' vast numerical superiority. Still, the Taino held out until the Spanish succeeded in capturing their cacique, Cotubanama, who had retreated to a small island off the coast. With the capture of Cotubanama, who was transported to Santo Domingo and publicly hanged, the rebellion in Higüey collapsed. Large numbers of the Indians fled to the mountains, while others ventured in their bark canoes across the treacherous and shark-infested Mona Passage, which separates Hispaniola from neighboring Borinquén, as the Indians called Puerto Rico. Most gave themselves up to the Spanish and resigned themselves to being parceled out as part of the encomienda.

Settlement of Higüey proved somewhat more difficult for the Spanish than its conquest had been. Because the Indians had reported that the area contained little or no gold, the Spanish had shown small interest in its settlement. At Ovando's orders, Ponce, using mainly Indian labor, oversaw the construction of two towns there, Salvaleón, on the coast, and Santa Cruz de Aycayagua, which was farther inland. He also administered the distribution of land and Indians to

Mounted Spaniards battle Indians in a 16th-century illustration. Though the Indians of Hispaniola vastly outnumbered the Spaniards and fought valiantly, they could not cope with their enemies' horses, dogs, crossbows, and firearms.

settlers in the province. Labor and property in Higüey were distributed according to the established custom of Hispaniola: settlers received a plot of land in town on which to construct a house and a *caballería* in the countryside for farming. (A caballería equaled approximately 33⅓ acres.) Depending on the settlers' social and marital status, they also received anywhere from 30 to 80 Indians as laborers, with hidalgos receiving more than commoners and married men more than bachelors.

Ponce's commitment to settling on Hispaniola, as opposed to exploiting it for the short term, was demonstrated most obviously in Higüey by the large stone house he had the Indians construct for him in Salvaleón. The only one of its kind in the province, it indicated that its owner anticipated living in the New World for a long time, perhaps permanently. It spoke as well of his status as the acting governor of the region. The vast majority of the houses lived in by the Spanish on Hispaniola at the time consisted of mud walls with a thatched roof. Such design was adequate for the island's climate and suited the needs of most of the "settlers," who still intended or hoped to return to Spain.

The transient nature of the settler population was reflected in Higüey. By 1506 land grants and the encomienda had been used to entice an estimated 100 families to the region, mainly to the environs of Salvaleón, but within two decades that number had dwindled to 15. Many of the immigrants had not returned to Spain, however, but to potentially more prosperous regions in the New World discovered by subsequent Spanish exploration. News of gold or silver was always a spur to settlement, and Panama and Mexico proved to be especially popular sites.

Though he maintained his farm and home in Salvaleón, Ponce de León was among those who were inspired by reports of gold to explore the lands nearby Hispaniola. As a member of Columbus's second expedition, he had presumably been among the first Europeans to lay eyes on Borinquén, the smallest of the island group (the others, in order of size, are Cuba, Hispaniola, and Jamaica) known as the Greater Antilles. And as the most powerful resident official of Higüey he was certainly aware of the regular commerce between the Indians of his province and those on Borinquén's west coast, which lies just 80 miles to the east across the Mona Passage. According to Oviedo, it was as a result of this trade that Ponce learned from the Indians of Higüey that there was much gold on Borinquén.

(Borinquén, the Indian name for Puerto Rico, is still often used in various forms by its inhabitants to designate the island and its people. Puerto Rico's national anthem, for example, is called "La Borinqueña." Columbus, who first saw the island on November 19, 1493, named it at that time San Juan Bautista, after Saint John the Baptist. After Ponce de León's voyages there, the Spanish began referring to the island as San Juan Bautista de Puerto Rico. The last two words mean "rich port" and refer to the beautiful harbor Ponce discovered on the northern coast that today serves the island's capital city, San Juan. Over time, San Juan came to refer solely to the city of that name, and Puerto Rico to the island, which today is a commonwealth in association with the United States.)

With Ponce dutifully reporting news of Borinquén's supposed riches to Ovando, the governor in 1506 organized an armada for the island's exploration, with Ponce as its commander. Very little is known about this first Puerto Rican expedition of Ponce's, primarily because great pains were apparently taken to keep it a secret, even from King Ferdinand (Queen Isabella had died in 1504) and the officials of the royal

court in Spain. Knowing that discovery, conquest, and
settlement could lead to the kind of position and
privileges Columbus had enjoyed, would-be explorers, governors, and admirals competed for the court's
favor, schemed against one another and guarded maps,
geographical information, tips, and hearsay as if they
were gold.

Ovando would have had good reason for secrecy,
for by appointment of Ferdinand he was the governor
general of all Spanish claims in the New World (which
as yet still really amounted to no more than the island
of Hispaniola, the only site where settlement had
proceeded to any effective degree). As such he was
well aware of the welter of claims and counterclaims
surrounding his own position and authority and thus
would have been likely to proceed with caution on
any further matter of exploration in the New World.

The most serious of these involved Diego Columbus, the great explorer's son. By the terms of the
Capitulations, his original agreement with the Crown,
Christopher Columbus was to govern all the lands
that he discovered in the course of his voyage. But
because of his mismanagement of the Spanish colony
on Hispaniola, Columbus had been recalled to Spain
in 1500 by Ferdinand and Isabella and refused permission to return to the island. The monarchs were both-
ered less by his mistreatment of the Indians than by his
heavy-handed governing style, which had incited virtually all the Spanish settlers on the island to a state of
almost perpetual rebellion. Led by Francisco Roldán,
the colony's chief justice, some had even made
common cause with the Indians. (That Columbus,
by birth a Genoan, was considered by many settlers to
be a foreigner did not aid him in commanding their
loyalty.)

Deciding, in Ferdinand's words, that Columbus
was "a good admiral but not a good viceroy," the

The ruins of the mansion that Columbus built for himself at Santo Domingo. Though a brilliant seaman, Columbus was a poor administrator, and his brutal style of governing caused widespread discontent on Hispaniola.

monarchs dispatched one of their most trusted officers, Francisco de Bobadilla, to right the situation on Hispaniola. Bobadilla was granted almost absolute power to carry out his mission. He arrived at Santo Domingo on August 23, 1500, and was treated almost immediately to the sight of a couple of corpses swinging from the gallows; they were, in Las Casas's words, "still fresh, having been hung just a few days earlier." Questioning Diego Columbus (the elder), who had been left in charge while his brothers hunted rebels in the interior, the horrified Bobadilla learned that five more rebels were to be hanged the next day. The ringleader of the most recent uprising had escaped this fate: Columbus had ordered him flung into the sea from the top of a watchtower. That was all that Bobadilla needed to hear. He clapped Diego into irons and arrested Bartholomew Columbus and the admiral himself as soon as they returned to Santo Domingo. The humiliated discoverer of the New World was

A depiction of Columbus in prison, following his recall to Spain in 1500. Francisco de Bobadilla succeeded Columbus as governor of Hispaniola.

shipped back to Spain in chains while Bobadilla took his place as governor of Hispaniola.

Though he was allowed to make one more expedition to the New World, Columbus would never set foot on his beloved Hispaniola again. "Of Hispaniola . . . and the other lands I never think without weeping," he wrote not long before his death in 1506, and his oldest son, Diego, was no less regretful over what had been lost. Even before his father's death, he had begun petitioning the Crown for the restoration of all the privileges to which he was hereditarily entitled by virtue of the Capitulations.

As Bobadilla's successor, Ovando was regarded by Columbus and his heirs as a usurper. Hopeful of increasing his wealth and influence by engaging in further exploration, such as that which he commissioned Ponce to perform in 1506, Ovando would have been keenly aware that any benefits deriving from Ponce's discoveries on Puerto Rico would likely be claimed by Diego Columbus as rightfully his. Thus he had every reason for secrecy.

Apparently, Ponce first sailed for Borinquén from Santo Domingo in late 1506 at the head of a small fleet of five ships, which probably carried a little more than 200 men. The fleet made land somewhere on Borinquén's west coast, probably not far from either of the present-day cities of Mayagüez or Aguada, where at Ponce's orders his men made contact with the local Indians (who were also island Arawaks, or Taino). Relations between the two groups were friendly at this point, most likely because the Borinquén natives were well aware, as a result of their contact with the people of Hispaniola, of the power of the Spanish and were thus eager not to antagonize the newcomers. The Spanish also promised to help them fend off the frequent raids of the more warlike inhabitants of other nearby islands, the Caribs, some of whom also lived in the easternmost portions of Borinquén.

After several days of feasting, with the Spanish liberally plying the Indians with wine, the Indians responded to Ponce's entreaties to direct him to a better harbor for his ships. With the Indians acting as guides and porters, one group of Spanish traveled overland to the present-day site of San Juan, while the ships made their way along the coast, first northward and then eastward. Once the Spanish had established an encampment, they set the Indians to the task of gathering gold. Samples of the precious metal were sent back to Ovando with a couple of the ships while the remaining explorers went with the Indians to establish mines at various locations. In a short time, however, having demonstrated the potential richness of Borinquén, all the Spanish returned to Hispaniola. In all likelihood this initial expedition had been conceived purely as a voyage of preliminary exploration, with no intent of founding a permanent settlement.

Made secure by the friendly reception the Indians had given his first expedition, Ovando apparently felt that the show of force that had been presented on Ponce's first expedition, with its five ships and 200 men, was sufficient to overwhelm Borinquén's native population into passivity, for when Ponce sailed for the island again in July 1508 he commanded just one caravel and 50 sailors and soldiers. Two great storms nearly cost him his small ship en route; twice the vessel was driven onto the rocks, nearly foundering, and the men were forced to jettison many of its supplies to keep it afloat. Having sailed north and then east from his landfall on Borinquén's west coast the first time around, on this voyage Ponce headed first for Isla Mona, an islet in the Mona Passage where a farm had already been established for the provision of cassava bread to the settlers. Then he set sail almost due east. In several weeks' time he thus coursed along the length of Borinquén's south coast before trending northward along its easternmost extension and then westward back along the northern coast to the accommodating harbor at San Juan. Combined, the two voyages thus constituted a circumnavigation of the island. Though Ponce presumably made a chart or

The death of Columbus in Valladolid on May 20, 1506. The great explorer passed his last years in embittered obscurity, continually petitioning the king of Spain for greater recognition and more financial reward.

some kind of record of its coastline, no such document has been discovered.

Ponce's commitment to the New World as a place of permanent residence did not mean that he was uninterested in making a fortune there. At the harbor near Caparra, as the Spanish initially called the village they established near the site of present-day San Juan, Ponce had his men build a huge hut (to be used as a warehouse for supplies and trade goods), a causeway and dock, and several roads. Farther inland, the village itself was established. Ponce's house here was less grand than his stone dwelling in Higüey on Hispaniola. His Caparra home, which he described as "moderate," consisted of whitewashed mud walls, with a terrace and a battlement, surrounded by some sort of fortification. At night it was illuminated by torches that hung from several strategically placed cressets. Nearby, the Indians were forced into service clearing land and establishing farms for Ponce, King Ferdinand, and the village. After Ponce, as acting governor of Puerto Rico, had established a steady food supply for the colony—until the first harvest, he sent regularly to the Spanish farm on Isla Mona for food—and arranged for the distribution of Indians to the settlers, he turned his attention to gold.

Both Ponce and his king profited from his exploration and settlement of Borinquén. Through Ovando, Ponce negotiated an agreement with Ferdinand whereby he was essentially granted a license to mine gold on the island. As was true of most such permits for exploration and development that the Spanish Crown granted following Columbus's initial voyage, the person seeking permission for the enterprise in question—Ponce, in this case—was expected to bear all the costs of the endeavor. Ponce therefore had to pay all the expenses necessary to mine gold on Borinquén—mainly food and supplies for his labor

force, which consisted of Indians and Spanish. The
king then took the customary royal share: one-fifth of
all the gold mined. What remained was then divided
in half, with the Crown taking one share and Ponce
the other. Ponce thus received 40 percent of the gold
taken from "his" mines, minus his costs. Though this
arrangement was obviously more favorable to Ferdinand than it was to Ponce, the profits from gold were
still sufficient to make Ponce an extremely wealthy
man by the standards of his time and place. His farms,
both in Higüey and Caparra, were also profitable, and
he was probably additionally rewarded by his monarch
for his successful establishment and management of
several royal agricultural projects on Borinquén.

For the Spanish, gold made Borinquén an attractive prospect for settlement, and Ponce encouraged
newcomers by persuading Ovando to intercede with
Ferdinand to allow him to grant licenses to individuals
to mine the precious metal. Such individuals were
granted a greater number of Indians and subsidized
with cassava bread rations. Control over such disburse-
ments made Ponce an extremely powerful man on the
island. Those who received such licenses were expected, of course, to grant the king his one-fifth share;
presumably, Ponce also received some sort of financial
compensation, probably in the form of his own share,
for granting such licenses. By October 1510 he had
completed work on his most ambitious project, a
foundry for the smelting and refining of gold in
Caparra.

As on Hispaniola, the labor for most of these
projects was performed by the Indians, who were
subjected to all the same abuses that the natives of the
first settlement of New Spain had endured. It did not
take the natives of Borinquén long to rebel against
such treatment. Within months, according to Oviedo,
the Indians of the island, particularly in the west and

The port of San Juan, Puerto Rico, from an engraving made in 1671. In 1506, Ponce de León led the first Spanish invasion of the island of Puerto Rico, also called Borinquén, in an effort to find more gold.

the south, discussed the idea of rising up in concert against the Spanish. (Made more fearful of the Caribs by their closer proximity to them, the Indians farther east were more inclined to resign themselves to Spanish domination in exchange for promises of protection.) They were held back, however, by the belief that the Spanish were immortal. It should be remembered that the arrival of the Spanish was no less of a shock to the worldview of the Indians than the discovery of the Americas was to the European consciousness. Initial belief that the newcomers were gods was not uncommon among the native peoples of the New World.

Oviedo maintains that the Indians decided to resolve the issue by experimenting on a single Spaniard to learn if in fact he was able to die. A cacique named Urayoan, whose domain was in the western part of the island near a small Spanish settlement named San Germán, made plans to waylay a solitary colonist as soon as the opportunity presented itself. When a lone Spanish wayfarer named Salcedo approached the village, a small group of Indians materialized and offered to ferry him on their shoulders across a river. In midstream they suddenly seized him and held him under the water until he drowned. Still concerned that he might possess godly powers, they dragged his corpse to the shore and kept vigil over it for several days until the stench convinced them that decomposition had begun.

Now sure that the Spanish were as mortal as they, the Indians began in earnest to plan their uprising. In the northwest part of the island the most powerful landowner was a man named Cristóbal de Sotomayor, an ally of Diego Columbus and a notorious abuser of the Indians. Not surprisingly his estates became, in the early months of 1511, the first target of the rebellion. Though Sotomayor had been informed by Ponce himself that his behavior was causing great unrest among the Indians, he persisted with his abuses, eventually growing so arrogant that he ignored a specific warning from a Spaniard fluent in the Taino language that an attack was to be launched on his property. Only this interpreter survived the onslaught that followed.

As on Hispaniola, the Spanish response was swift, sure, and brutal. With Ponce taking personal command of the Spanish forces, the rebellion was quickly

An early illustration of the various ways in which the Spanish made the natives of the New World work for them. Within a half century, the Spanish virtually wiped out the entire Indian population of Borinquén.

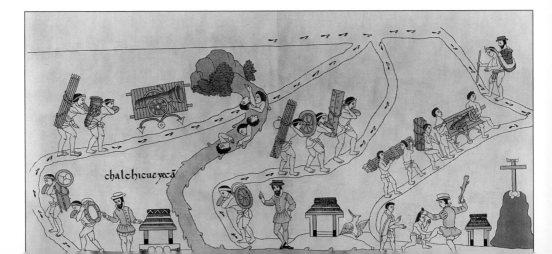

put down, and the destruction of the Taino proceeded in a manner akin to what had taken place on Hispaniola. By this time Ponce had imported a great many animals—goats, pigs, sheep, horses, cattle, and others—from Hispaniola and Spain. Among these immigrants to the New World were greyhounds, which the Spanish quickly found useful for terrorizing and hunting down the Indians. On Puerto Rico, one of Ponce's own dogs, a red-pelted, black-eyed creature named Becerillo (Little Calf), became legendary for his purported ability to sniff out a single hostile native amid a group of friends. According to the 16th-century Spanish historian Antonio de Herrera y Tordesillas, "the Indians were more afraid of 10 Spaniards with the dog, than of 100 without him." Becerillo proved so valuable that he earned from his master a crossbowman's pay as well as gold and slaves. The exploits of Becerillo and his canine friends led to the coining of a new Spanish word in the New World—*aperrear,* which means "to cast to the dogs."

In such fashion, Ponce presided over the subjugation of Borinquén, where the demise of the Indians was as rapid as on Hispaniola. Estimates of the island's Taino population at the time of the first Spanish settlement vary widely, anywhere from 30,000 to 300,000. In a very short time, however, the Indians' numbers were much easier to count. Diminished by Spanish oppression, disease, and cultural disintegration, the Indian population on Borinquén had been reduced to an estimated 4,000 by 1515. By that time there were so few natives left on Borinquén and Hispaniola that Ponce and other officials there had asked for and received permission to kidnap natives from other islands and bring them to the Greater Antilles as laborers. In 1544 a Spanish bishop counted 60 Indians remaining on Puerto Rico, and those few were gone just a short time later.

CHAPTER
SIX

TO LIVE FOREVER

Like Columbus before him and many conquista-dores to follow, Ponce found it easier to defeat the native peoples of the New World than to master the intrigue of colonial politics. Ponce's savvy as an administrator never matched his mettle as a conquistador. By 1511 the Crown had seen fit to honor Diego Columbus's inheritance in the New World, and the new Admiral of the Ocean Sea (the title was inherited as well) took Ovando's place as viceroy of the islands Christopher Columbus had originally discovered. On Hispaniola and Puerto Rico he immediately installed his favorites in political office. As a protégé of Ovando, Ponce was naturally viewed as a potential rival and was regarded with suspicion by Diego Columbus—especially as he had once seen fit to jail two of Columbus's appointees for Puerto Rico, Juan Cerón and Miguel Dias de Aux—and the feeling was mutual. In 1511, at Ferdinand's order, Ponce was officially replaced as governor of Borinquén by Diego Columbus.

On Borinquén, Ponce's followers and allies resented the accession of the Columbus faction, and their dissatisfaction grew when the newcomers began asserting their power. As on Hispaniola, the single greatest source of power on Borinquén was control over the distribution of Indians through the encomienda or *repartimiento* (a similar system of forced labor). As governor of the island, Ponce had overseen the encomienda, but now Diego Columbus's men

Ponce de León's men searching for the fountain of youth. It is not entirely clear whether Ponce believed that such a fountain existed, or if he used the legend to entice an aging King Ferdinand into supporting his further expeditions.

87

began redistributing the Indians among their favorites. Colonists who lost their Indians or received a diminished share were understandably angry, as control over such labor was critical to amassing wealth, and Ponce's supporters suffered the most under the new government. Events in Spain had made it politically necessary for Ferdinand to agree to the younger Columbus's restoration, but the king remained grateful to Ponce for his many loyal services, and he made it quite clear that he did not want him to suffer political revenge at the hands of the Columbus faction. Even so, Ponce had some of his property seized, including (temporarily) the stone house in Higüey and a ship, and he seems for a time to have been confined to a kind of house arrest on Borinquén.

Though Ponce retained certain titles and privileges on Borinquén—the king awarded him control over a fort overlooking San Juan harbor, for example, and he remained captain of the island, meaning that he was its highest military authority—it is not surprising that under such circumstances someone of such a restless nature would begin to look for new opportunities elsewhere. So long as the Columbus faction remained in power, life on Borinquén was likely to be difficult for Ponce, who showed no special interest or skill in the kind of politicking necessary to protect his interests. He was notably resistant, for example, to returning to Spain to lobby the court, the king, and his counselors, a tactic frequently used by colonial officials embroiled in political disputes. Even when in 1512 Ferdinand offered him a magnificent opportunity to argue his case by personally summoning him to Spain for a royal audience, Ponce tactfully declined.

It is not clear whether the idea of Ponce's making a voyage of expedition to the Bahamas (the chain of many small islands stretching to the northwest of

Hispaniola) initially came from Ferdinand or Ponce himself. In either event, such an expedition would have suited the interests of both men. Ponce was looking for new opportunities to enrich and advance himself, which a voyage of discovery would surely offer. Such a voyage would also allow Ferdinand to reward Ponce while resolving the political dilemma on Borinquén. Ponce would be removed, but with the prospect of finding an equally desirable situation for himself on some newly explored island, perhaps Bimini, as the Spanish referred to the island in the Bahamas that had most attracted their interest. (Bimini is today the name of two very small islands, measuring just nine square miles in all, off the lower east coast of Florida, separated from the mainland by the Straits of Florida. The Spanish used the term, however, to refer to a mythical island of unspecified location that they had heard the Indians speak of, and, by extension, to the entire Bahamas chain, of which they possessed at the time only the scantest geographical knowledge.) And whatever discoveries he might make among these new islands would not be open to challenge by the Columbus family, whose claims did not extend to the Bahamas.

There was apparently one more powerful incentive for such an expedition, but whether it appealed most to Ponce or to Ferdinand is unknown. The first specific mention that Ponce's aim in exploring the Bahamas was the discovery of a fountain of youth comes in a 1514 letter from Pietro Martire d'Anghiera to Pope Leo X. Known in English as Peter Martyr, d'Anghiera was a diplomat who represented the pope in the Spanish royal court; he possessed a keen interest in exploration and would eventually become a member of the Council of the Indies, the Spanish government body responsible for overseeing New World affairs. (It was d'Anghiera who first used the term

"New World" to refer to Columbus's discovery.) The letter provided Leo with a brief account of Ponce's explorations in the Bahamas, which had taken place the previous year. Ponce "explored and investigated among the farthest countries an island called by us [Bimini]; there is a fountain continuing throughout the year that is so remarkable, that the water of this fountain being drunk makes old men young," d'Anghiera wrote. Still, it is not certain whether this fountain was originally one of the objects of Ponce's search and thus a reason for his expedition, or whether he heard of the phenomenon in the course of his voyage and reported its purported existence afterward to his king.

Anthony Devereux, for one, argues that Ferdinand, not Ponce, had greater reason to be interested in a fountain of youth. Dynastic quarrels in Spain had made it imperative that Ferdinand father a son by his new bride, Germaine de Foix, in order to keep his grandson, Charles, from inheriting his kingdoms of Aragon and Naples. But Ferdinand and Germaine had been unable to have a child together, and according to d'Anghiera, various potions and recipes prepared to aid conception had instead rendered the king impotent. At the same time, his overall health began to show a marked decline. By this logic, says Devereux, it was the aging, failing king (Ferdinand was 60 in 1512) rather than Ponce (still vigorous in his thirties, if one accepts the 1474 birthdate) who would have had the greatest interest in locating the site of the legendary restorative waters. There is no concrete evidence, however, that Ferdinand knew of the purported existence of the fountain of youth before he approved Ponce's Bimini expedition, or that if he did, he specifically charged Ponce with its discovery. Ferdinand did display much interest in having Ponce reveal "the secrets of these islands," as he put it, but the term "secrets" was commonly used in the 16th century in the context of exploration and referred more to geographical information—especially mineral and natural resources—than to the existence of mysterious phenomena such as the fountain of youth.

The modern reader might find it incredible that either Ponce or Ferdinand could believe in the existence of a fountain (the most common description, though some versions of the legend refer to a spring, pool, stream, or river) whose waters, if one bathed in them (or, in some versions, drank from them) restored the bather or imbiber, no matter how old, to the full bloom of youth. But there were many European tales about such a fountain long before Ponce's day. The

The legend of the fountain of youth goes all the way back to the 4th century B.C., when Alexander the Great conquered much of the known world. Alexander was reportedly told by a quartet of giants that the miraculous fountain sprang from the Garden of Eden.

most common accounts belonged to the vast store of legend and mythology that had grown around the figure of Alexander the Great. The historical Alexander was king of Macedon (now part of Greece) in the 4th century B.C.; a military genius, in just 10 years' time he expanded his domain from the Balkan peninsula to include virtually all of Eurasia, from modern-day Turkey eastward to the Himalayas and present-day India, as far north as the Black and Caspian seas, and as far south as much of present-day Egypt and Libya. For medieval Europeans, Alexander was a romantic as well as a historical figure, and the real-life story of his empire building had been embellished by any number of popular fanciful legends that featured his encounters with improbable beasts and otherworldly opponents—sea monsters, giants, dog-headed creatures of the desert, and the like. One of the most enduring tales in the Alexandrian romances concerned the fountain of youth, which was fed by waters from the Garden of Eden. Its existence and location was supposedly divulged to Alexander by four horned giants, each of them 14 feet tall, that he encountered en route to India.

The fountain legend had other roots in the European tradition as well. It was supposedly among the wonders in the many-splendored kingdom of Prester John, the fabulously wealthy Christian monarch who was said to rule somewhere among the infidels in the lands beyond the known world. Though Prester John was a fiction he was widely believed in, and more than one expedition was sent by European monarchs in search of his kingdom. To the people of Europe, whose knowledge of and access to the outside world was limited, such tales did not seem all that fantastic. Geographical knowledge was hard to come by, and with each new discovery by the likes of Columbus and Hernán Cortés, even educated Europeans seemed

According to a later legend, the fountain of youth was located in the kingdom of Prester John, pictured here. Prester John was supposedly the Christian ruler of a mythical land somewhere beyond the known world.

to be called upon to completely revise much that they had "known" to be true about the world.

The discovery of the Americas thus seemed to make the existence of such a phenomenon as the fountain of youth even more likely. If a whole new world could be found, why not a fountain of youth? Indeed, after Columbus's voyage, many of the mysterious but still undiscovered places in which Europeans believed were now placed somewhere in the New World. For example, Christian dogma held that the Garden of Eden was a real place that existed somewhere on the globe. Tradition set its likely location in the Middle East somewhere near the Tigris and Euphrates rivers, but on his third voyage Columbus became absolutely convinced (and reported as much to Ferdinand and Isabella) that he had located it in the Gulf of Paria, which separates the island of Trinidad from the northeast coast of Venezuela.

At some point, Ponce apparently received information from the Indians that led him to believe that a fountain of youth could be found in a place or on an island called Bimini, but it is unclear whether the Indians had their own myths about restorative waters or if they simply responded to Spanish inquiries on the subject, as they often did, by telling their interrogators what they wanted to hear. (It is also possible that the ambitious Ponce did not really believe such reports but passed them on to Ferdinand anyway, with the knowledge that such information would spur the king's interest in Bimini and make him more likely to approve a voyage of exploration there.)

In any event, when Ponce eventually filed a formal application with the king for permission to explore Bimini, he was careful to list less speculative benefits that the Crown would gather from his expedition than a fountain of youth, namely new lands and additional slaves. Ferdinand's approval arrived in the form of a contract dated February 23, 1512. Like all such contracts between conquistador and king, the document contained explicit stipulations on everything from mineral rights to the distribution of land and Indians and the structure of future municipalities. Under an arrangement known as the *adelantamiento,* Ponce was to be awarded civil and criminal jurisdiction over the new lands he discovered for the rest of his life, but he was expected to outfit the expedition at his own expense.

The adelantamiento was a system of licensed entrepreneurship that could be traced back to 12th-century Castile, the homeland of Isabella, a region of Spain that had once been an independent kingdom.

Adelantados first acted as magistrates, or agents of the king, but their powers expanded during the Moorish wars, when Spain's monarchs awarded titles and rich frontier estates in exchange for loyal service. If a noble could defend the land he could profit from it. In the New World the system guaranteed maximum gain and minimum pain for the Crown. In exchange for certain incomes and monopolies, adelantados assumed the costs and risks of exploration, conquest, and defense. Within a generation or two, all titles and privileges reverted back to the monarchy.

Ponce de León departed from the port of San Germán on March 3, 1513. Although his log of the voyage has been lost, Antonio de Herrera y Tordesillas supposedly consulted it in compiling his account of the voyage. About 60 people probably sailed with him, an approximately equal number of sailors and *gente de*

An engraving from 1591 showing the houses and settlement of a typical group of Florida Indians at the time of Ponce de León's arrival.

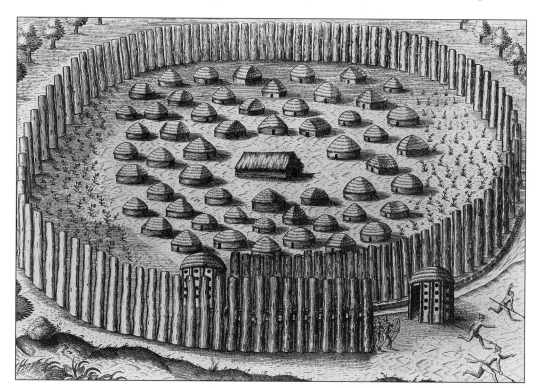

tierra (people of the land), as soldiers and farmers were referred to. At least one man, Francisco de Ortega, brought his wife, Beatriz Jiminez, who in turn was accompanied by her sister Juana. At least two Indian slaves sailed with the expedition, presumably because they had some knowledge of the Bahamas or of the Indian languages spoken there. Two free blacks also sailed as members of the crew; these men had probably come to the New World as slaves with their Spanish masters and then been given their freedom.

Diego Bermúdez, brother of the discoverer of the island of Bermuda, skippered the lead caravel, *Santiago*. Bermúdez was assisted by the 31-year-old chief pilot, Antón de Alaminos, a native of Palos, the Andalusian port that had supplied the manpower for Columbus's first voyage. (Some scholars believe that Alaminos had served as a ship's boy for Columbus.) Juan Bono de Quexo, an old friend of Ponce's, captained the triangular-sailed *Santa María de Consolación,* and Juan Pérez de Ortubia was at the helm of the two-masted brigantine *San Cristóbal.* All but the last ship belonged to Ponce himself. He had ordered a brigantine, like the other ships, from Spain, but since it did not arrive in time, he requisitioned one that usually ferried between Puerto Rico and Hispaniola.

The ships set a northwest course through the Bahamas. One day, less than a month after skirting the Turks and Caicos Islands, stopping briefly at Guanahani (San Salvador), Columbus's first landing spot in the Indies, and sighting Great Abaco Island, the fleet anchored in eight fathoms of water off a previously uncharted coast. The next day Ponce rowed ashore to take possession of this land for Spain. Lush groves of grey cypress, tulip, ash, and magnolia trees, backed by tall palms and broom pines, exuded a delightful bouquet. Azaleas, oranges, and jasmines were in bloom, and the woods were alive with the droning of insects and the calls of hummingbirds, loons, and wild turkeys. Because Ponce de León had made his discovery during the season of the Catholic holy day of Easter, which the Spanish called Pascua Florida, or the Feast of Flowers, he called this new land Florida. Although in making his landing Ponce became (in the belief of some scholars, who discount reports of an earlier Viking discovery) the first European to set foot on the continent of North America, he believed, as would many explorers in the years to come, that Florida was an island. Using an astrolabe, the forerunner of the sextant, to compute the altitude of the stars, the fleet's navigators had determined the ships' position to be about 30 degrees north latitude. A faulty instrument or out-of-date tables probably distorted that reading, however, and most scholars place Ponce's landfall somewhere farther south, between present-day Daytona Beach and New Smyrna Beach on the east coast.

On April 8 the three ships set sail once again, to the north at first, just briefly, then south following the shore. Two weeks later the Spaniards spotted some huts, the first sign they had seen of Indians. The next day they encountered a current strong enough to offset the favorable wind that filled their sails. When the two ships closest to the shore dropped anchor they strained at their moorings; the brigantine, unable to resist the current's force, drifted out to sea and was lost to its sister vessel for two days. Although Ponce had no way of knowing it at the time, this current—the Gulf Stream—was as important a find as Florida. From its origins in the Gulf of Mexico, the stream passes through the Straits of Florida and shoots up the southeastern coast of the United States until it meets a cold current off Cape Hatteras, North Carolina; then it flows northeastward into the Atlantic Ocean. Years later, Alaminos charted a course for cargo vessels bound for Spain that used the 50-foot-wide current,

which averages 4 miles per hour, to speed them on their way.

For the present, the conquistador and explorer was more interested in the Indians who had appeared and were motioning him ashore, but when he complied the natives wounded two of his men with bone-tipped arrows and tried to seize his longboat. The Spaniards retreated and sailed south to a river that was probably somewhere near Jupiter Inlet. While they gathered wood and water and waited for the *San Cristóbal,* another party of Indians attacked. This time the explorers fared a little better in the skirmish, and Ponce captured one of the attackers to train as an interpreter and guide.

On Sunday, May 8, the ships rounded the tip of Florida, which Ponce named Cabo de las Corrientos (Cape of the Currents) after the forceful current. The next week they passed a string of small islands (the

This engraving depicts Florida Indians performing a religious ceremony. In 1514, the Spanish Crown granted Ponce the authority to colonize Florida and convert the Indians to Catholicism.

Florida Keys), which they dubbed Los Martires (the Martyrs) because the rocks resembled suffering men. Navigating the shallow waters around the keys taxed Alaminos; to avoid running aground, he posted a lookout for changes in water color and heaved the sounding lead over the side to check the depth. At night such careful navigation was impossible, and the ships were forced to anchor.

In the Marquesas Keys, Calusa Indians wearing palm-leaf loincloths canoed across an inlet to trade animal pelts and guanin, a low-grade gold. To the great surprise of the crew, one of them spoke Spanish, taught to him either by slave traders or by ship-wrecked sailors. When the bargaining soured, the natives seized the anchor cable of one of the ships and attempted to tow the vessel away. In the ensuing struggle the Spaniards captured four Indian women, who indicated that a chief named Carlos had gold to sell. Following the captives' directions, the mariners steered north up the west coast to the vicinity of present-day Charlotte Harbor. On June 11 Carlos greeted the Spanish, but with 80 canoes of archers, not precious metals. Neither side, however, got close enough to inflict injury on the other.

Three days later, having had no luck in finding gold, Ponce ordered his fleet to turn around. The ships veered west to the Dry Tortugas, where the men, dazzled by the abundant wildlife, killed 160 giant sea turtles, numerous seals and manatees, and thousands of gannets and pelicans. Trying to follow the directions of an Indian captive, Ponce then directed the flotilla eastward. In the Bahamas once more, the untrust-worthy *San Cristóbal* foundered, but the men of the other two ships managed to rescue its crew.

Although the explorers had sipped sweet water from springs on various islands and even the North American mainland, Ponce had not succeeded in locating the fountain of youth. He decided to head home in the *Santiago* but instructed Ortubia and Alaminos to continue the search in the *Santa María*. On October 10, 1513, a little more than seven months after he had left, Ponce returned to Borinquén. His scouts returned in February, having discovered the island of Bimini but not the secret of eternal youth.

For Ponce, however, there certainly seemed to be enough time to secure his claims to the lands he had discovered (particularly magnificent Florida), colonize them, and add to his fortune. To that end he sailed for Spain in early 1514, seeking Ferdinand's formal approval of his colonization plans. He brought for the king 5,000 gold pesos from his personal coffers, which surely made Ferdinand more agreeable to his proposals. On September 27, 1514, the two reached an agreement for the colonization of Ponce's new lands. Under its terms, Ponce was to attempt to convert the natives to Catholicism, but if they resisted, "he may make war on them, capture them, and take them for slaves." Ponce was to have the sole right to profit from the slave trade and other commerce on these new islands unless he granted other individuals a specific license to engage in commercial activity there. The agreement also specified the taxes Ponce was to pay to the Crown on his activities—one-tenth for the first five years, gradually increasing to the customary one-fifth—and even went into detail on such matters as the dimensions of the houses he should build.

Ponce's hasty departure for Spain almost immediately following his first Florida expedition indicates his eagerness to exploit his discoveries, but events would conspire to prevent him from immediately acting on his settlement plan. With Carib raids on Borinquén and Hispaniola persisting, an armada was organized to put an end to them, and Ponce was asked to serve as its commander. He did, with some success,

This 20th-century illustration shows an aged Ponce sipping the waters of a Florida stream, hoping that he had at last discovered the fountain of youth.

although he also endured the most ignominious episode of his career when a Carib ambush forced him to abandon a shore party of soldiers and washerwomen on the island of Guadeloupe. He was further delayed by Ferdinand's death in early 1516, which resulted in an intensification of the political power struggle on Borinquén. As a result, Ponce felt compelled to return once more to Spain in order to secure his prerogatives. He spent at least 18 months in Spain between 1516 and 1518, and, according to some sources, married a woman named Juana Pineda. It is assumed that Ponce's first wife, Leonor, died sometime before the second trip to Spain, probably in early 1516.

On a second expedition to Florida in 1521, Ponce's party was attacked by Indians, and he was wounded by an arrow in the thigh. Though his men succeeded in carrying him back to his ship, he died of his wounds on the island of Cuba.

Even less is known about Ponce's second Florida expedition than about his first. Whether he still hoped to locate a rejuvenating fountain is uncertain, but he certainly paid attention to the practical details essential to the successful settlement of Florida. His two caravels, which left Puerto Rico in February 1521, carried somewhere between 80 and 200 people, including priests to attend to the colonists' spiritual needs and establish missions for the conversion of the Indians. They were stocked as well with seeds, horses, livestock, and other equipment and supplies necessary for the establishment of a self-sufficient colony.

Ponce's route is unknown, but he apparently made land somewhere on Florida's west coast, most likely in the vicinity of Sanibel Island. There, he and his men began constructing a settlement, but disease and Indian attacks quickly thinned their ranks. Although later European visitors and settlers in the region reported the Indians to be essentially friendly, they were nowhere near as peaceful as the Taino, and Ponce, as a

This statue of Ponce de León in present-day St. Augustine, Florida, commemorates the Spanish explorer's role in the history of the New World.

veteran conquistador, was in the habit of using strong-arm diplomacy. The Indians responded in kind, and in the course of one of many battles between the uninvited newcomers and the inhabitants, Ponce was seriously wounded by an arrow in the thigh. Infection set in. His men shipped him off for treatment to the nearby island of Cuba, the nearest Spanish settlement, but there was little that could be done, and he died in July 1521. "Here rest the bones of a Lion / mightier in deeds than in name" read the words of the epitaph later composed for this most mysterious of explorers by the poet and historian Juan de Castellanos.

Ponce's personal quest for immortality was at an end, but the objects of his search continue to inspire travelers. The 27th of the 50 United States, Florida is today one of the nation's fastest-growing states, annually attracting hundreds of thousands of "explorers"—some of them tourists, some of them settlers—who have come in search of the same things that brought Juan Ponce de León: wealth and restored youth. (As a result of its Spanish heritage, Florida also remains linked, culturally and politically, to the Caribbean and Latin America.) These later explorers are more likely to have been attracted by jobs, the availability of land, or visions of sunshine dancing off the placid waters of a sandy beach than by the prospect of finding gold nuggets in a rippling stream, but all those who have been rejuvenated by the state's year-round sunshine and languorous climate would find it hard to believe that the fountain of youth is not still to be found there somewhere.

CHRONOLOGY

c. 1474	Born Juan Ponce de León in San Tervás de Campos, Spain
1492	Christopher Columbus sails west across the Atlantic Ocean, hoping to reach the Indies; lands on the island of San Salvador in the Caribbean Sea; makes landfall on Hispaniola and Cuba and claims these territories for Spain
1493	Columbus returns to Spain as a hero
1493–96	Ponce signs on as a common foot soldier in Columbus's second voyage to the New World; Columbus and his men lay claim to numerous islands and develop a colony on Hispaniola; Ponce takes part in fighting between Spaniards and Indians
1500	Columbus is replaced as governor of Hispaniola and placed under arrest; returns to Spain in chains
1502	Ponce marries Leonor, a Spanish-born woman, and becomes a prominent citizen of Santo Domingo, Hispaniola
1504	Nicolás de Ovando, governor of Hispaniola, appoints Ponce to lead a Spanish expedition against rebellious Indians in Higüey; after successfully concluding campaign, Ponce becomes deputy governor of Higüey and

oversees the construction of two towns, Salvaleón and Santa Cruz de Aycayagua

1506   Columbus dies in Valladolid, Spain, on May 20; Ponce commands expedition to explore the island of Borinquén

1508   Ponce undertakes second voyage to Borinquén; establishes settlement at Caparra and becomes acting governor of Borinquén

1511   Puts down rebellion by Borinquén Indians

1513   Sets out on voyage of exploration to the Bahamas; lands on the coast of Florida

1514   Signs contract with Spanish crown setting out terms for settlement and exploitation of Florida

1521   Undertakes second expedition to Florida; is wounded in battle with Florida Indians; Ponce's men remove him to Cuba, where he dies in July

FURTHER READING

Devereux, Anthony Q. *Juan Ponce de León, King Ferdinand, and the Fountain of Youth*. Spartanburg, SC: Reprint Company, 1993.

Dodge, Stephen C. *Christopher Columbus and the First Voyages to the New World*. New York: Chelsea House, 1991.

Lawson, Edward W. *The Discovery of Florida and its Discoverer Juan Ponce de León*. St. Augustine, FL: St. Augustine Historical Society, 1946.

Morison, Samuel Eliot. *The European Discovery of America: The Southern Voyages*. New York: Oxford University Press, 1974.

Sale, Kirkpatrick. *The Conquest of Paradise: Christopher Columbus and the Columbian Legacy*. New York: Knopf, 1991.

Stefoff, Rebecca. *Ferdinand Magellan and the Discovery of the World Ocean*. New York: Chelsea House, 1990.

———. *Vasco da Gama and the Portuguese Explorers*. New York: Chelsea House, 1993.

INDEX

Adelantamiento system, 94–95

Alaminos, Antón de, 96, 97, 99, 100

Alexander the Great, 92

Arawak Indians, 61, 79

Asia, 17, 18, 32, 37, 38, 39, 43

Atlantic Ocean, 17, 30, 97

Aztec Indians, 16

Bahamas, the, 88, 89, 90, 96, 99

Becerillo, 85

Bermuda, 96

Bermúdez, Diego, 96

Bimini, 89, 90, 94, 100

Bobadilla, Francisco de, 77, 78

Bono de Quexo, Juan, 96

Borinquén. *See* Puerto Rico

Calusa Indians, 99

Cão, Diogo, 45

Caonabo, 58, 61, 65

Caparra, Puerto Rico, 81, 82

Capitulations, the, 47, 76, 78

Caribbean Sea, 20, 53, 57, 104

Carib Indians, 79, 83, 100, 101

Carlos, 99

Castellanos, Juan de, 104

Cathay. *See* China

Catholicism, 28, 33, 54, 55, 59, 64, 65, 100

Cerón, Juan, 87

Chanca, Diego Alvárez, 57

Charlotte Harbor, Florida, 99

China, 16, 31

Columbus, Bartholomew, 30, 64, 77

Columbus, Christopher, 17, 18, 20, 21, 22, 30, 32–35, 37, 45, 46–49, 51, 52, 53–54, 55, 56–59, 62, 63, 65, 68, 75, 76, 78, 81, 87, 90, 92, 93–94, 96

Columbus, Diego, 76, 77, 78, 79, 84, 87, 88

Columbus, Ferdinand, 59, 64

Conquistadores, 16, 20, 67, 87, 94, 104

Cortés, Hernán, 16, 20, 92

Cotubanama, 72, 73

Council of the Indies, 89

Cuba, 53, 104

Cuneo, Michele de, 60, 63

da Gama, Vasco, 45, 46

d'Anghiera, Pietro Martire, 89

Devereux, Anthony Q., 26, 90

Dias, Bartolomeu, 45

Dias de Aux, Miguel, 87

Dominica, 57
Dominican Republic, 53, 56
Dry Tortugas, the, 99
Encomienda system, 63–64, 73, 87
England, 30
Enterprise of the Indies, 33, 45, 48
Ferdinand (king of Spain), 16, 22, 26, 28, 29, 32, 33, 34, 35, 37, 45, 46, 47, 48, 49, 53, 54, 57, 65, 75, 76, 81, 82, 87, 88, 89, 90, 91, 94, 100, 101
Florida, 15, 53, 89, 97–100, 102, 104
Florida Keys, 99
Fountain of youth, the, 15, 16, 22, 26, 89, 90, 91–94, 99–100, 102, 104
France, 30
Granada, siege of, 29–30, 33, 37
Great Abaco Island, 96
Guacanagari, 65
Guadeloupe, 57, 101
Gulf of Mexico, 97
Gulf of Paria, 94
Gulf Stream, 97
Haiti, 53, 58
Henry the Navigator (prince of Portugal), 42–44, 46
Herrera y Tordesillas, Antonio de, 85, 95
Hidalgos, 51, 54, 74

Higüey, Hispaniola, 71, 72, 73, 74, 75, 81, 82, 88
Hispaniola, 48, 49, 71–74, 76, 77, 78, 79, 81, 82, 84, 85, 87, 96, 100
    settling of, 51–69
Indians. See Native Americans
Isabela, Hispaniola, 59, 60
Isabella (queen of Spain), 16, 22, 26, 29, 32, 33, 34, 35, 37, 45, 46, 47, 48, 49, 53, 54, 57, 65, 75, 76, 94
Jamaica, 53
Japan, 32
Jiminez, Beatriz, 96
Jiminez, Juana, 96
João II (king of Portugal), 32, 33, 45
Jupiter Inlet, Florida, 98
Las Casas, Bartolomé de, 53, 55, 56, 59, 65, 66, 67, 68, 77
Leo X (pope), 89–90
Lesser Antilles, 57
Manoel I (king of Portugal), 45
Marco Polo, 30, 31
Mexico, 16, 74
Montserrat, 57
Moors, the, 26, 29, 37, 46
Native Americans, 15, 53, 56, 58, 59, 61, 71, 74, 81, 83, 84, 88, 94, 96, 98, 103
    and European diseases, 68–69

exterminated by
Spanish, 67–69, 85
and slavery, 48–49, 61,
62–64, 65, 69, 73, 87, 96
Navidad, Hispaniola, 58, 59,
61
Nevis, 57
New World, 16, 19, 21,
22–23, 25, 29, 31–32, 51,
52, 53, 56, 58, 59, 67, 69,
74, 76, 77, 78, 81, 83, 85,
87, 89, 90, 93, 95
Núñez de Guzmán, Pedro,
27, 28, 29
Ocean Sea, 30, 31, 32, 34
Ojeda, Alonso de, 59
Ortega, Francisco de, 96
Ortubia, Juan Pérez de, 96,
100
Ovando, Nicolás de, 56, 65,
71, 72, 73, 75, 76, 78, 79,
80, 81, 82, 87
Oviedo, Fernández de, 27, 28,
29, 67, 75, 82, 83
Panama, 74
Ponce de León, Count Juan,
26, 27
Ponce de León, Isabel
(daughter), 71
Ponce de León, Juan
Bahamas, explores, 89–96
birth, 25, 26
Carib Indians, campaigns
against, 100–101
childhood, 27–29

and Columbus's second
expedition, 20, 49,
51–56, 75
death, 104
Florida, discovery of, 15,
96–100, 102–4
and the fountain of
youth, 15, 16, 22, 26,
87–89, 90, 99–100, 102,
104
Granada, campaign to
capture, 29–30
Higüey, Hispaniola, acting
governor of, 73–75
marriages, 71, 101
Puerto Rico, conqueror
and governor of, 21,
75–87
Taino Indians, campaigns
against, 71–73
Ponce de León, Juana
(daughter), 71
Ponce de León, Juana
Pineda (second wife),
101
Ponce de León, Leonor (first
wife), 71, 101
Ponce de León, Luis (son), 71
Ponce de León, María
(daughter), 71
Ponce de León, Rodrigo, 26,
29
Portugal, 16, 30, 32, 33, 37
age of discovery, 42–46
Prester John, 92

Puerto Rico, 21, 53, 57, 73,
    75, 78, 79–85, 87, 96, 100,
    101, 102
Roldán, Francisco, 76
St. Kitts, 57
Sale, Kirkpatrick, 62
Salvaleón, Hispaniola, 73, 74
Sanibel Island, Florida, 103
San Juan, Puerto Rico, 75, 79,
    80, 81, 88, 96
Santa Cruz de Aycayagua,
    Hispaniola, 73
Santangel, Luis, 47
San Tervás de Campos, Spain,
    26
Santo Domingo, Dominican
    Republic, 56, 71, 72, 73, 77,
    79
Sauer, Carl, 62
Slavery, 43, 48–49, 53, 61,
    62–64, 65, 69, 73, 87, 96

Sotomayor, Cristóbal de, 84
Spain, 20, 21, 22, 25, 26, 30,
    34, 37, 49, 51, 52, 53, 56,
    61, 62, 65, 74, 76, 78, 85,
    88, 90, 94, 95, 96, 100, 101
Spice trade, 39–42, 46
Straits of Florida, 89, 97
Taino Indians, 61, 62, 64, 65,
    66, 67, 68, 69, 72–73, 79,
    84, 85, 103
Talavera Commission,
    33
Trinidad, 94
Tristão, Nuno, 43
Urayoan, 83
Venezuela, 94
Venice, 17, 37, 41–42,
    46
Viking explorers, 31, 97
Virgin Islands, 57
Watts, David, 61

SEAN DOLAN has a degree in literature and American history from SUNY Oswego. He is the author of many biographies and histories for young adult readers, including *James Beckwourth* and *Magic Johnson* in the BLACK AMERICANS OF ACHIEVEMENT series, and has edited a series of volumes on the famous explorers of history.

RODOLFO CARDONA is professor of Spanish and comparative literature at Boston University. A renowned scholar, he has written many works of criticism, including *Ramón, a Study of Gómez de la Serna and His Works* and *Visión del esperpento: Teoría y práctica del esperpento en Valle-Inclán.* Born in San José, Costa Rica, he earned his B.A. and M.A. from Louisiana State University and received a Ph.D. from the University of Washington. He has taught at Case Western Reserve University, the University of Pittsburgh, the University of Texas at Austin, the University of New Mexico, and Harvard University.

JAMES COCKCROFT is currently a visiting professor of Latin American and Caribbean studies at the State University of New York at Albany. A three-time Fulbright scholar, he earned a Ph.D. from Stanford University and has taught at the University of Massachusetts, the University of Vermont, and the University of Connecticut. He is the author or coauthor of numerous books on Latin American subjects, including *Neighbors in Turmoil: Latin America, The Hispanic Experience in the United States: Contemporary Issues and Perspectives,* and *Outlaws in the Promised Land: Mexican Immigrant Workers and America's Future.*